THE LOVE BETWEEN
MY THIGHS

The Scarring of More Than A Woman's Heart

Tiphane` L.M. Purnell

TLM Publishing

Publisher's Note
This is a work of nonfiction. It depicts, portrays, and represents real people, places, and events. An effort was made to recreate events, locales, and conversations from the author's memory of them. In order to maintain anonymity in some instances, names of individuals, places, identifying characteristics and details such as physical properties, occupations, and places of residence have been changed. All rights reserved, including the right of reproduction in whole or part of any form.

Library of Congress Control Number: In publication data
Copyright: @2017 by Tiphane` L.M. Purnell
ISBN: 978-0-9996663-0-2
Cover Design: Shawn J. Moore | Blueprint Media Design | info@shawnjmoore.com
Edited by: Author Jonathan C. Harris | Shamika Cook | Terri Champion
Formatted by: TLMason | Fiverr
Author: Tiphane` L.M. Purnell

Ordering Information:
Special discounts are available on quantity purchases by corporations, associations, and others. For details, contact the publisher. For orders by U.S. trade bookstores and wholesalers contact the publisher at TLMPublishing.LLC@gmail.com.

Printed in the United States of America.

DEDICATION

To my Mom,

You birthed the strongest love from between your thighs,
and built her into a uniquely and wonderfully made Queen.
Because of you I walk with my head higher, stand taller,
endure longer, pray harder, achieve greater and love others
with a heart of gold like yours.

TABLE OF CONTENTS

ACKNOWLEDGMENTS

All the glory belongs to you oh God! In this year, I have relived some of the most horrible accounts of my life to produce a massive testimony for women and men around the world. But as with all great things, life hit me and it distracted me. This past summer, I got another wind and picked my book back up. It felt like an internal war to release this book, especially since my "blissful" relationship was crumbling. I would like to thank all of the men and women out there who have a story to tell, but are silent in their suffering, because you all inspired me to write for you.

To my dear friend Shawn Moore, thank you for taking my vision and creating amazing graphics for my book, logos and marketing materials. We will continue to support Blueprint Media.

I want to send a huge thank you to Katchan "K.D." Harris

for being an amazing mentor throughout this entire process. You continued to push me through my motivated and unmotivated days until I reached the greatness that you knew was in me to produce through writing.

To my only sibling, my twin, Michael A. Purnell II and his lovely wife Ryan M. Purnell. I love you both. Michael, thank you for being my very first best friend and for understanding me when nobody else would or could. Thank you Ryan for bringing Khalil into my life at a time when I needed it most and loving me through one of the darkest seasons in my life. The love from you both helped me overcome, and find the words to produce that chapter of my story.

A special thank you to those who edited (Shamika Cook, Author Jonathan C. Harris), provided suggestions, and most importantly, encouraged me to the finish line.

Lastly, I want to thank Mr. Michael A. Purnell Sr. and Mrs. Patricia L. Purnell, my parents. Without you there would be no me. You created me together and groomed a fearless, unique and wonderfully made Queen. You have supported me in every vision, business venture, career decision, and move. And now you are supporting me in my journey as an author.

PROLOGUE

This was me, a valued prize stuck in a see-through box. Love for me was like a crane claw game. Growing up they had one at my local Pizza Hut, but you could find them in most restaurants or any video arcade, supermarket, restaurant, movie theater, bowling alley or shopping mall. For those of you who don't know what this game is, walk down memory lane with me. The crane claw is made up of a window made of glass or a cheaper material such as acrylic on all four sides of the square shape machine. The crane claw consisted of prizes visibly seen through this glass window that lured gamers to play to win. Prizes usually consisted of plush toys, jewelry, hats, balls, dolls, shirts, candy and electronics. More expensive prizes are sometimes placed in a plastic bag so the prize is harder to pick up. Although the prizes were all in the same glass machine, they were all of different values. Some of you see where I am going with this. After the player inserts money into the machine (normally a quarter or two), they can manipulate the joystick that controls the claw for a certain amount of time. During this time, the player is able to move the claw back, forth and sideways using the joystick to manipulate the direction. Once the player has positioned the claw over the prize they want, they press a trigger button on the joystick that descends the claw and makes an attempt to grip the prize. Once the grip is attempted, the claw ascends back into the air and makes its way towards an opening in the corner of the case. If the player is successful, the prize will be released from the grip of the claw into the opening and dispensed through a chute into a hatch for the player to retrieve. However, for most of us that have ever played this game in our lifetime, we know that majority of the people who played are unsuccessful in retrieving a prize from this machine. As a child this game was so enticing because we wanted all the prizes in this glass machine. I say we because I am included. I use to jump up and down and beg my dad to give me more money so I can try again, but even the small fee (or so I thought back then) of a quarter was too much money for my parents to see the value to keep investing. To our failure of retrieving the prize and running out of money to play, our parents forced us to walk away, thus settling for a less enticing substitute.

This was me! Men would see me from afar, be excited in the beginning about the enticing prize before their eyes, put money into me (like the machine), then play the game to try to win me over. Some of you don't see the problem in that, but stay with me. You see men are gamers by nature. In my life, many have invested their fifty cents. The crane claw would start moving upon their control. They would line it up just right over top of me, then press the trigger button to descend and pick me up. We would both be excited – me because I thought I was finally someone's prize, and them because they got what they wanted (or so they thought). The crane claw would slowly ascend back into the air, but before it could get to the opening in the corner of the machine to drop the prize down the chute for the person on the other side to retrieve, it would loosen its grip and the prize would release back into the masses of the other prizes. At this point, there are two choices to make; 1. invest more money and try again, 2 walk away and settle for losing. Most would walk away because the investment was low risk...I mean it was only fifty cents, so the investment didn't hurt. They walk away as free as they were when they walked up. They had nothing to lose when they walked away, but I (the prize) had lost from the very beginning. I was the one stuck in a see-through box far before he walked up to the machine to play, barred internally, yet everyone could see me. Each time a new player came, I was so excited to be chosen that my overcompensation of giving my all started long before he even gave more than fifty cents. I endured the clinching of the metal teeth from the crane claw digging into my body, and tightening its grip to pick me up into the air. I was excited about the adventure of being suspended in the air (even though I am afraid of heights) because I was willing to give of myself. The small frame of time I spent suspended in the air above the masses, I made it count! Only to have fifty cents invested in me and be controlled by a joystick from the outside looking in. I soon realized that my heart was just as transparent as this window box of various prizes. I was preyed upon for way less than a prize – I was a pawn. There I was, back in the masses, beat up from the trip on the crane claw that I thought would set me free, only to be back where I started. Feeling alone, even though there are plenty of other prizes barred in that machine with me. Feeling stuck between wanting to be free to stand on the other side of that window, or wanting to hide and bury yourself even deeper into the masses.

How many fifty-cent men or women have come into

11

your life? And you sat there hoping that this time would be the last because it wasn't about the money, it was about the love. And when I say it was about the love, I'm talking about the one that you wanted to build together.

We are all born kings and queens, but it is up to you whether you want to be crowned or not. You have to fight your way to the thrown. Your experiences build your steps to the thrown. The obstacles you overcome give value to the title. Your wisdom gives you the confidence to reign supreme. I was nervous to release this book until that thought whispered into my heart and took over my subconscious mind in the cool, quiet hours of the early morning. Re-writing my story helped me release the scars that surfaced beyond my heart and embedded pain in my mind and soul. I was tired of reliving the hieroglyphs of my past, so I decided to climb the steps towards my crown of freedom.

INTRODUCTION

*T*he windows of life have forsaken me
The pain is unbearable; the last thing on my mind
is to get down on my knees
My heart is heavy, feels like someone died
I have always hated my life so much everything I am I tried
to hide
How could you do this, I'm so angry I just want to leave
But I can't leave my mom behind, she is my best-friend, a
true Queen.
You couldn't see her beauty, her smile, and the way she
gives selflessly to anyone in need?
My mom is a rare light that some people are too blind to
see
Her perfection, her skin, her soul is a goddess
My heart wants to stop beating for her pain
This is the worst day of my life, but you thought her cry
was in vain

A 911 call for help from her is on repeat in my mind
I cried myself to sleep while she sat in the dark confined
Staring out the window trying to deal with my pain, while
you were dying inside.
Why did this happen to you? I only knew this in movies to
be true!

I entered the world peeking my head between the thighs of the strongest, most beautiful woman in the world. The ultimate unconditional love; next to God. Somewhere in that cloud 9 of unconditional love, my ideology of love shifted over the years. Through the clouds of dusts from accidents and explosions, I found that once all of that fades there is so much more on the other side. What shaped my outlook on love? An intentional conscious of self-discovery. Uprooting the layers lying beneath the soiled surface. The core is metaphorical to the soul, and the soul is the core of life where all facets of the being grow from spiritually, mentally, emotionally, physically and psychologically. The soul is where the origin takes place and the roots manifest growth from there. My root came from my parents as most do. Before I came out of the womb the path of grief and doubt had begun. It stemmed from my soul before I even met this earthly kingdom we call the world. Generations of loveless hurt, cheating, and confusion embedded deep within the roots of the family tree that nobody could explain. The grief that pieces together the hurt of current generations, and will continue to infect our bloodline like an untreated leech, sucking the blood dry from each and every vein. My job is to be the breech. Like hacking into a brain, but instead, hacking the entire bloodline for change. Working backwards to reverse the corrupted cells and get back to the soul, plant new seeds and grow an unbreakable harvest. How do I plan on doing this you ask? By leaving it all on this book as the saying "leave it all on the track." The only way I could think to share where my ideology of love, grief and doubt came from was to put my pen to paper. I have unveiled many aspects of my hidden life in these chapters. The journey I endured of uprooting what was in order to plant the seed of what is and see the harvest of what will become was not easy. Some people will read my book and judge me. Some will read it and know they aren't alone...whatever feeling is provoked I'm ready for it ALL! I'm not perfect and neither is my testimony. Stay with me as my heart unfolds on the pages to come, while you release the scars of your own and find satisfaction in the healing that will come. This is my story.

1

The Beginning

We all have scars. Some are physical and some are emotional, but both have a process to heal. Not all scars are visible, even if they are physical. Scars are hidden under clothes, embedded in our hearts, consume our minds and damage our souls. No matter how many times we are scarred, our bodies are programmed to heal, but the healing process for each scar differs. Growing up in church, they hid scars well and taught me to do the same.

I don't get it. I come from a two parent home, raised in church, loving family, but I was still empty. My dad was in the home. I mean I grew up a daddy's girl, but I was still missing something...I was empty. I just always felt like something was missing. I was good, but I wasn't great. I looked good, but I wasn't beautiful.

I know you're thinking there is an easy solution.

Beauty starts from within right?

Love starts with self-love right?

Yea...I thought the same. I thought that all the Hour of Powers, Youth nights, revivals, Sunday services, etc. were pouring self-love into me. I mean I was learning God's love and surrounded by church folk, so why did I still feel empty? What was missing?

I loved being around my church family and learning how to walk in love, but I started wondering when was I going to feel it. I was young and had no idea what I was even supposed to be looking for or what I was missing, but I was headed on a journey to discover the very thing that plagued my thoughts and emotions from a young age.

Surprising for some I know. My parents were ministers. My brother and I were well dressed and well mannered, my dad the minister of music...we had a better life than most.

I'm starting to sound ungrateful, right? I mean I was loved so what was the problem?

The older I got it hit me. I wanted my dad's attention more than ever. I developed quickly. The fat girl that everyone bullied as a young girl was turning into the thick chick that every teen wanted a piece of. Thick thighs, spreading hips, full breasts and a bright smile. I was thick like the boys liked it, but I was bigger than the rest of the girls so I felt fat...tall, fat and out of place. But for some reason it wasn't hard for me to get attention. The attention just wasn't enough though. I was longing for something more. I just couldn't get past my flaws.

I remember having friends that longed for the relationship I had with my dad. He attended all my games, helped with my homework, and taught me how to drive. Yet the attention from men older than me who appreciated my newfound curves as sexy and not fat captured my attention more. It filled the void I thought I was missing. I was tired of the cheerleaders and the smaller girls getting all the guys I found attractive. I knew I looked pretty, but I didn't feel it, so I felt like I needed to do more. If only I knew then what I know now...but this is the story of life.

My soul was uprooted on January 31, 2015 when I received the call that I never imagined in my 27 years of life. It was a clear, yet cold winter afternoon my mom and I had a conversation no different than any other day about life and guidance. You ever hang up the phone with someone and they call you right back, and you pick up thinking they forgot something, but they butt dialed you? Well, that happened to me that day. Only, I never saw the call come through, so I didn't pick up at all. And then a call rang through on my boyfriend's phone. The call was dark, cold...the kind where you witness a loved one take their last breath. Unbeknownst to me that's what was happening. The right and left sides of the heart that I witnessed in bliss my entire life were no longer working together, and the two veins that pump the blood into the heart clotted that day (heartbroken). It was on that call that I realized she had died...inside. Broken hearted, shattered to the core. Wanting nothing more than to be dead because her heart had failed her. Hearing screams of her pain on the call that day remain hieroglyphic thoughts that I cannot shake. I use to dread the thought of having to face that day, but it's even worse when you're dead, yet alive and there is nothing that can be done to be a saving grace. For a second my blood circulation stopped with hers. Trying to find the air to gasp and collect myself.

I was use to being my mom's saving grace, but trying to drive, collect myself and speed to her rescue wasn't exactly working out. I couldn't hang up on her, so I had my boyfriend at the time keep her on the phone while I frantically dialed my brother's cell. My hands were shaking, the traffic was crazy and I had passed every exit possible to access the interstate from route 13 in order to reach her destination in North Wilmington (Delaware). "Why was this happening to me?" My brother finally picked up...thank God because he was a lot closer than I was. The entire way there all I could think about was this is surreal. A blissful day with the love of my life became one of the darkest days of love in my life in the matter of seconds.

2
My First

Everyone has a first, whether it is a first love or a first sex partner. They embed their position in your life as your first. The first to kiss you with passion. The first to lie to you. The first to take your virginity. The first to show you a great time. Our first heartbreak is usually our biggest lesson. Sometimes it's even our biggest pain. Mine was no different. He was my first. The one who gave me the nickname "Ocean." The one who took my virginity. The one that lied to me. And the one that broke my heart. This was the start of my journey of the *Love Between My Thighs* that I was seeking. But from the beginning, I was left broken with nothing except the bodily fluids he left seeping and the title of "My First".

We were young...still in high school when we met. We also attended the same church. He was tall, slim, caramel complexion, bright smile, nice cut, etc. He was nice looking, but his annoying personality made him unattractive. I was far from interested. I worked hard on my image in high school and I did not want to be seen with him. My brother was a senior when I was a freshman, so I had a great start, and now that I was a senior, senior class president and well liked, I wanted to uphold that. My plan didn't work though. His persistence wore me thin. He was the first to open my eyes to my welcoming heart, both a strength and a weakness for me. Always seeing the good in everyone and being willing to give everyone a chance, even if my heart was on the table.

I would love to tell you the play by play of how I fell for him, but there are far more juicier details to share.

We officially became a couple, and he became even more annoying than he was before. He showed up at my classes, cracked corny jokes, had no swag at all (lol), but he was tall and handsome, so that was a start. We started showing up everywhere together in school and church and he seemed to be trying to find his way to the "cool kid" side of life.

The more time we spent together, the closer we became. I remember talking about lying in the back of pickup trucks and watching the stars at night. You know the corny young love conversations that made you get butterflies.

We continued to grow and so did our youthful hormones. I was never the one who wanted to lose my virginity before marriage, but he was experienced already, so you know how that influence goes. He became my first sex partner on my birthday, October 3, 2004. I lasted until my senior year of high school with everyone making fun of me that I was still a virgin. I thought that I would go to college, be low key, get married young and do it God's way. It sounded good, but the flesh felt better.

I don't know what it was about me, but for us to be so young, his family seemed really embracing. His mom and step dad would talk about us being together long term, and they were really happy for us. His mom offered to cook dinner for me on my birthday at their house. She really put her heart into the menu. She asked me for a list of all my favorite foods and made sure she had them on the menu. I really didn't care about anything but the macaroni and cheese. Oh and I had to make sure BBQ sauce was in the house. I need that anytime I eat someone else's food. It's my salt and pepper.

After dinner we took a ride in my 1996 two-door, green Pontiac Sunfire on a trip to get an ice cream cake from Dairy Queen. Of course we took a detour. He had a way with his mouth, in more ways than one and that was the only alone time we would get on my birthday. We pulled into a dark parking lot on Christiana Road. I parked under a tree in the darkest area we could find. I turned the car off and looked at him. He drifted closer to me and kissed me softly on my lips then made his way to my neck. That was my spot. An electrifying feeling ran through my body and sent a tingling feeling to my feet and pulsated my clit. "I can't do this," I whispered in his ear. He ignored me and kept French kissing my neck and groping my body. The flesh felt good and I completely disregarded my want to save myself until marriage. I made it to my senior year of high school. Everyone knew I was a virgin since that awkward conversation in English class. But I was getting weaker each second that passed. We climbed into the back seat, slid the front chairs all the way up and folded them down. The position was a little tight for his 6'0 body to maneuver, but he made it work.

I laid on my back with my head on the hard interior of

the side of the car in the backseat. He lifted my thick legs up and placed them on his shoulders. As I braced myself for what was about to happen, I felt the ocean between my thighs flowing heavier, my flesh getting weaker, and my breaths getting shorter as he inched his thickness into me. It was hard for me to be disappointed at this point. I was already in too deep now, so what was the point in stopping. He continued moving his hips to a rhythmic beat inside of me. He slowed down to lean down and kiss me. As he started massaging my oceanic juices, he leaned up with his thickness still inside and asked "Are you ok?" I replied "Yes" with a soft moan of satisfaction, yet slight hesitation. He lifted my thick mocha chocolate thighs and pulled me down lower in the seat, spread my thighs and entered deeper into my wetness. I didn't know what I was doing, what I was supposed to be feeling, and the setting wasn't the most comfortable or romantic. While he was stroking I looked into his shiny brown pupils and asked "Are you all the way in"? A big no no I know (well I know now, but I didn't at the time). It wasn't all it was cracked up to be. And since I ruined the mood, that was the end of that moment. We drove back to the house in silence.

The next week our youth pastor called a meeting with my parents to discuss me and Andre's relationship. It was weird sitting in the office space behind the front desk of the church in between both of my parents, sitting across from my youth pastor. He told my parents that he observed how close Andre and I had gotten and asked me if we were in a relationship. When I confirmed that we were, he suggested that we end it. He told my parents that he was known for hitting girls and having sex. My parents were shocked and wanted to end our relationship, but I didn't judge him. I never judged because "church folk" had judged me all through my teen years. I had my own car that I was paying for, and I was following my own mind and heart, so I kept seeing him.

The meeting with my youth pastor led to a deeper conversation with my parents around sex. The night we got home my mom asked me if he and I had been intimate. It was hard to open up to my mom because the look she gave could burn a hole through your heart in less than a second flat. I finally told her that we had sex…without a condom at that. Her heart dropped, but I could tell she was fighting back anger because she wanted me to be comfortable talking to her.

I stayed away from Andre for a while, but I decided to go visit him one night when his mom wasn't home. I came straight from work so I was tired. We chilled for a while, but you know what happens when two teenagers are alone with raging hormones. He left his brother in their room and led me towards the couch in their living room. He pushed me gently into the recliner chair and made his way toward me slowly. He began kissing my neck. He slid his hand under my shirt and began to squeeze my breasts and newly erect nipples. My pussy started to twitch and I felt myself getting wet. As he laid on top of me continuing to kiss my body, I noticed his dick had thickened through his pants and he was ready for the next step. He started unbuckling my pants and lifted up my wide hips to slide them down over my butt and thick thighs. As he slid his finger up my vagina to unleash the ocean of fluids that accumulated from our foreplay, he bit his lip as his eyes connected with mine. He entered into my abyss and we were once again connected.

In the middle of being intimate, a knock came to the door. We ignored it and stayed in tune with each other. A female voice yelled through the door,

"Andre! Open the door! I know you're in there!"

My mood was interrupted as I started trying to figure out who the heck this chick was, but he must have taken the comment from our last encounter to heart because his thickness seemed much deeper and satisfying this time.

The knocks continued and so did we. Eventually there was silence and we were back in our zone, but the knocks triggered his brother. Shortly after his brother started calling out for him, the knocks started on the back door.

"Andre! Why are you treating me like this? I know you are in there with that girl! I thought you loved me. I just want to talk!"

She continued banging on the door and screaming his name. At this point his brother was now yelling, I was mad, and the mood was ruined. This chick was not leaving, but somehow I had to go home, and he needed to handle that. I put my hands on his chest and pushed him off of me. It got quiet again as I made my way to the bathroom to adjust myself and put my clothes back on.

I don't know what he did to this chick, but now she was back at the front door. Knocking angrily from the front door to the back door quickly became annoying, but even more a sticky situation when it was time for me to go. Andre and I began arguing about how I was going to leave the house without something popping off, but of course he was standing there looking at me with the dumb guy look of "Oh crap I'm caught". I went out the front door and headed to my car, but of course she confronted me before I could even get past the front step. She started yelling, but I wasn't for it. I went to walk away, but I noticed her fist was already balled up. As I went to walk away, she swung.

Although I dodged the full impact, my glasses were knocked off my face and she must've had keys or something in her fist because I had a light scratch across my face. After that it was a wrap. I don't even know what happened, but I know anytime my glasses get knocked off my face it's game over. I remember a crowd of people surrounding us and her being on the ground. By the time we got up, Andre was gone and the cops had been called.

My glasses were broken and all I could see were shadowed silhouettes of my surroundings. With no spare pair in sight, I didn't know how I would make it home, or how I would explain to my mom that my glasses were broken. I jumped in my car and made my way down route 40 to the route 1 ramp and finally to the Lens Crafters at Christiana Mall. Thankfully they were able to repair my glasses. I made my way home thinking of the best way to get out of this. I figured what my parents didn't know wouldn't hurt them. That sounded good until the police knocked at the door.

There I was at the Wilmington (Delaware) courthouse over a boy. It's funny now because I realize how stupid I was, but at the time I swore he was the one I would spend my life with. I was fighting for our love, or so I thought. I should've just let him stay the annoying dude that I wasn't interested in.

They say the same way you get a man is how you will lose him, and that is exactly how we ended. I didn't know that's how I was getting him, but his ex tried to warn me. I should've listened to her, but he made it sound like she was the crazy one. I guess someone thought his dick game was good, because she was hooked in a crazy way.

We didn't see each other for a while after the fight and all the court stuff went down. Everyone on the block testified that the chick did have something sharp in her fist and that she attacked me, so I was good, but that was on her record. Christmas was the next thing coming up and even though we went through some stuff, I wanted to get him something. I mean, he was my first, and for whatever reason I felt connected to him in spite of everything. He told me he wanted a portable TV/DVD player. That was a popping thing back then. I remember looking up the price and thinking "Man this boy is expensive and I have a car note and bills!" But I searched for the best deal and got him what he wanted and a few extra things he needed. I kept seeing things while I was out at the store that I knew he needed to replace…like his ripped up wallet. This was the first time I realized what my love language was to him. I was a giver. Not just gifts though.

Andre was determined to make it up to me. He worked so hard to get me, so I guess he didn't want to lose me that easily. He didn't drive, but he always made a way to support me. The day of my senior fashion show, he came to support me and said his cousin dropped him off. I thought nothing about it because I was happy to see him. He helped me clean up at the end of the night and walked me to my car in the school parking lot. As we were walking, I noticed a jeep sitting idle with headlights on not too far from where I was parked. He looked at me, pointed and said, "That's my ride". As I looked into the jeep, I got a clear view of a female that I had never seen or heard about before. I had a gut feeling, but ignored it.

About a week later, we were at our church for an event. As we were all leaving, I noticed the same Jeep from my fashion show sitting out front waiting. After some words were exchanged in the lobby of the church, I found out that his "cousin" was actually his new girlfriend. He walked outside to greet her as she got out of the driver's seat. They exchanged a passionate kiss before he got into the driver's seat. I felt hurt because he lied to me, and I snapped on him and her. It was about to go down and everyone knew it, including the youth leaders. There were about four people holding me back. I was so out of character, but I didn't care. You know love (or lust should I say) will make you do some crazy things.

3

One-sided Love

Have you ever been in a relationship where you claim the relationship but the other person doesn't? Yea that was Karnell and I. I was naive to the game during this time. If I did anything for a man beyond friendship, I thought I was his girl. He would tell me that I was his, but save face in front of his friends. He was a cool kid with an image to uphold. The best way I can describe him is a younger, slimmer Morris Chestnut. Smooth deep chocolate complexion, bright white smile, and those eyes that sparkle off the reflection of the light and nice height.

I did the pursuing this time. He was already in the picture before Andre broke my heart because we worked at the same job. I noticed him only because he was the only black male in the Pharmacy and we were both young. I spent the time noticing him and trying to see if he noticed me. We never went to the movies, never went on a date, we only went to work, talked on the phone, and hooked up to have sex. I honestly didn't even think about that at the time. Sex and eating became my coping mechanism during this season of my life. I never knew that eventually both would spiral out of control.

I guess the car became a thing after my first because that's where we started. Then it became neighborhood cul-de-sacs, local parks, and parking lots. We were young and horny. I actually didn't even like sex, but after my relationship with my first (Andre), I was hurt and I thought that since I had already lost my virginity there was no going back in the church. The only difference this time was that I practiced safe sex. Giving more of myself became an addiction in hopes that if I gave what I had I would receive in return.

He got just as addicted to me as I was to him. Not in the way I wanted though, he only wanted my pussy. I guess he wanted things to be more comfortable because he got brave one day and invited me in his mom's house while she wasn't home. He was really horny that day. When he opened the door he greeted me with a soft kiss on my lips.

He took my hand and guided me to the back of the house where the living room was. We sat down on the couch and started kissing passionately with our tongues down each other's throats as far as they could reach and our hands gripping each other's bodies as hard as they could quench. He unbuckled his pants to let his erect dick loose as it was bulging through his jeans and restricted his passionate foreplay. He told me to take off my pants. As he helped me slide them down, his finger touched the wet spot on my panties from the ocean that flowed between my thighs.

He was heated and so was I. He wanted more of me this time, so he laid on the floor and said, "Come here". As I straddled my thick thighs on each side of his pelvis and squatted down to sit on top of him, he bit his lip and put his hands on my waist. I leaned forward slightly to allow his thickness to enter me, then sat back and began to ride him slowly. He started cursing and I could hear the sound of my wetness as I came down on his dick each time. I started gazing into his eyes, and for some reason that interrupted the moment. I don't know what happened, but the moment we connected, he changed positions. He told me to get up on my hands and knees with my back arched. He entered me again and began stroking me from behind. I could feel his balls hitting my wet pussy. I started to pop back slightly to try to find a rhythm. I still wasn't that experienced, but I knew I would try anything. It must've worked because he pulled out once he hit his climax. He didn't say anything though. He left me on the floor as he made his way to the bathroom to remove the condom. The way my pussy gets wet during sex I definitely couldn't move. He was taking too long though. I stood up. He came back as I was waddling my way towards the bathroom and said he wasn't done he wanted more...but I was done for the night. Even though he came, I was wondering why he abruptly switched positions. My mind got the best of me and I started thinking that he didn't really want to connect. He didn't want to see my face and make it special. He just wanted sex.

The next time Karnell and I hooked up was the last of our escapade. His mom was home, so we were back to the car, but this time we had a four door, so we had more room. I always heard of condoms breaking, but someone forgot to mention that they can also slide off and get stuck in your vagina. Well that was our luck this go round. He was trying hard to get it out, but I kept contracting my pussy muscles unknowingly, so it was making the condom slide deeper into my vagina. I started panicking because I knew for sure I was in big trouble this time. I thought I was going to have to go to the ER to get a condom out of my vagina...how embarrassing. Pulsating my vaginal walls wasn't helping at all. I had to concentrate. I ended up loosening my vaginal walls and holding it as long as I could to see if the condom would slide out. As I did that, Karnell said he could see the condom clearer. My oceanic juices made it very slippery, but he was able to grip enough of the condom to pull it out. We overcame stress, panic, and some serious teamwork to get it out, but we did. That was the last of our sex escapade. He said that he did not have time for any slip ups and no babies. I agreed!

We kept in contact on and off. I guess once he got to know me for who I was he said he actually enjoyed talking to me on the phone. His birthday was coming up and since I go hard for holidays and special events I wanted to do something special for him. I knew he had a collection of fitted hats and he loved Nike sneakers. He told me he didn't like balloons though. I ended up getting him a fitted hat to match a pair Nike sneakers. I wanted to give him his gift on his birthday, so I contacted him to stop by his house. When I pulled up he was with one of his boys. That was the first time we had been around other people since we hooked up. He didn't greet me with a hug or a kiss, which I thought was odd. I said hi to his boy and handed him the gift all hype. He loved it and told me thank you, but said he was getting ready to go. Even though he played it cool in front of his boy, he called me later that night to thank me again for the gift and we stayed on the phone for hours. I was so blinded by my excitement to give him his gift; I didn't even realize I was being played. Before we hung up the phone he told me that his mom was throwing a party for him at his house and she wanted me to come.

I had a gut feeling about the party, so I grabbed one of my girls to go with me. I had a couple friends with my same name, so I grabbed my hitter at the time and we rolled out. When we pulled up, we noticed a slim thick caramel complexion chick, wearing a dress that hugged every inch of her curves, giggling and flirting with Karnell holding a bouquet of balloons. She handed him the balloons and he kissed her on the cheek as I watched from the front window of my car. I zoned out for a minutes, but when I snapped back to reality, I heard my friend yelling from the passengers seat, "I'll get out and fuck her up right now, just say the word." I played it cool. I was still going to go inside, but only for a minute out of respect for his mom. That was even more awkward. His boys were all

38

over my friend, he didn't introduce me to anyone, and everyone was in their own click. I was uncomfortable. I felt out of place and I definitely didn't feel as pretty as the other girls that all the guys were drooling over. I was mad that he wasn't claiming me after all that we went through, but after that kiss outside, I can't say I was shocked. His boys invited my friend to an after party they were going to, but he didn't want me to come, so of course she wasn't feeling it.

We ended up leaving and having girl talk so I could let off some steam. I knew that his interest in me was over, but I was stuck with him as my prom date. If he could've backed out without getting grief from his mom he probably would have, but his mom was very involved.

Karnell and I were set to link up on a Saturday afternoon at the mall to get him fitted for my prom. On my way there, a car did an illegal U-turn in the middle of a major road and I totaled my car and suffered some pretty painful injuries. When I called Karnell, he sounded pretty nonchalant. With so much going on, I couldn't stand to think about him at the time, so I hung up, but if I didn't know before, I knew then that he didn't care about me.

Due to the accident, I missed time from school, and I thought that I was going to miss prom. Thankfully I recovered in time to attend, but I was still sore from the accident. His mom came to my house for the pre-prom activities and pictures, and then she came to my high school for the official pre prom event and our professional picture time slot. I wanted him to go to after prom with me, but he barely spoke to me during prom and on the ride home. He didn't even want to go to Denny's with me after. He was over it. Ready to get home and be with his friends away from me.

Even though we were over, his mom really liked me and wanted us to be together. She invited me to his graduation. I met at his house and rode with his family. I was proud of him, but I felt out of place. When he came out to greet his family at the end, he looked so happy to see everyone, but he didn't greet me with the same enthusiasm. He thanked me for coming and went on to take pictures with his family and some of his friends. There I stood with a disposable camera full of memories of someone who viewed me as just that...a disposable memory. A thought of the past.

Despite how I felt at his graduation, I invited him to mine. He was supposed to meet up with my mom, but she told me he never contacted her. His mom ended up texting my mom from his phone to tell her he slept through my graduation. His mother was furious. She made him stop by my house that night to give me my gift. I had a small gathering of family over to share their love and bring me gifts. He called me when he was outside. He didn't even want to come up to the house. As I walked down the driveway, I noticed that he was with his mom and they had driven her car. He didn't seem the least bit excited. He had the look on his face that you make as a child when your mom drags you out of the house. He got out of the passenger seat told me hi and said that his mom wanted me to have the gift. I was thankful for her. It was a Build-A-Bear with a white cap and gown and award metal around the neck, similar to an award I received my senior year. The birth certificate for my bear had my nickname at the time on it "Peachezz". His mom really paid attention to detail, which I admired because I was the same way. She told him that I was a good catch, but hey who really listens to their parents at that age.

Around that time, I went grocery shopping with my mom at a local store called Pathmark. Surprisingly, I ran into the girl from his birthday party that gave him the balloons. He didn't know it, but she and I attended the same middle school, so we knew each other. She was trying to explain herself in the middle of the floor in the

Seafood department, but all I could think about was him staring at her picture and gawking over her body with his boy right in front of me. He didn't know that we knew each other. Even if he did that wouldn't have change anything.

"Tiph I didn't know, you gotta believe me. He said ya'll weren't together" she said as I held back my anger. In my head I thought about fighting her, but what would that solve?

In the end, his new girlfriend ended up pregnant by him, and I ended up going to college. I was good, but this series of heartbreak over other women with "better bodies" than me led to a stream of insecurities hidden deep within.

4

True Love

While I was being played by the other two guys during my senior year, little did I know, I had the biggest secret admirer. Ya'll know what that is! That person that thinks highly of you, likes you more than a friend, studies your beauty, but does not reveal their identity to you. Yup, that's what he was, a 6'1 dark chocolate, stocky physique, bold in stature, but very quiet in personality. We attended the biggest high school in Delaware together at the time and out of a class of 700, we had three classes together...physics, business ethics and a study hall. I spent my days looking through him while he spent his studying me. It took me an entire year almost to notice him. As the senior class president, it

43

was my duty to get everyone to prom. One day in physics I found out he wasn't going and it crushed me. I started learning more about him. He worked a full time job, had a house and a newborn baby girl. I was impressed and humbled. I worked a job throughout high school, but I couldn't imagine having adult responsibilities at such a young age. I admired him. I spent the next couple weeks convincing him to go to prom, a once in a lifetime experience. I even invited him to my after prom getaway in Ocean City. I didn't realize it at the time, but after learning him, I became his helper. He started coming to study hall more just to ask me to help him with physics...we became physics partners. We sat close to each other in all 3 classes, not by choice, we had assigned seats.

Our bond grew, but a major event changed the trajectory of our relationship. My car accident. My car was totaled and the injuries from the fatality kept me out of school for weeks. The head trauma and body injuries were a threat to missing all of my senior events...from prom to graduation. While Karnell was nonchalant about these series of events, Derek was concerned if I was okay and asking my teachers when I would return to school. When I came back, my business ethics teacher was so supportive of my recovery. She was the one who told me that Derek was very concerned when I was out, kept asking if I was okay, and wanted to know when I would return. I didn't think anything of it at first, but I soon realized he had become my helper. At this stage everything was platonic, but I needed him. The tables had turned. Not only was he asking me about attending senior events, but he became my ride to the events. We spent the rest of the school year and the summer attending senior events and graduation parties together.

Life Jennings "Must Be Nice" and Bobby Valentino "Slow Down" rang through the speakers as we drove around with the top down, sun blaring and wind in our faces as we made our way to the graduation party that led our friendship to the path of a romantic relationship. The backyard had cleared out with only our friend's closest friends left behind, so we moved the after party inside. Dim lighting, couches and chill vibes, it was all couples in the room besides him and I. It didn't bother me one bit, but the agony of what I didn't know was killing him inside. We moved upstairs to the loft. And finally one of my friends just came out and said,

"He likes you...he's liked you for a while I don't know why you didn't notice!"

Probably because I was stuck on my exes. Sometimes

when you have something you want you miss out on what's in front of your face that you need. He liking me more than a friend was awkward, but it made sense after everyone broke it down to me.

1. He asked me to be his prom date. I turned him down in ignorance. I mean come on his daughter was only a couple months so there was no way (in my mind) he wasn't taking his baby mom to prom.

2. He became my driver. Literally and figuratively.

3. He held me down at after prom in Ocean city. It seemed weird because his baby's mom came, but the 3 of us hung out together when everyone else left us hanging and didn't answer their Nextel chirps. He was paying for his baby's mom stuff and mine, but innocent ole me just thought he was being nice.

4. All of our appearances together at every school event after my accident.

I got it! But I never looked at him that way. I just thought he was looking out for me because I looked out for him. Long story short we started dating. I met his daughter and started meeting his family. It got really weird the first time I rode with him to pick up his baby girl from his baby's mom house. He had a drop top Sebring, so it's not like I could hide. But she clearly knew who I was from prom and after prom. We won't even get into the drama that created...we would need another chapter for that. He had to move on though, so she had no choice but to deal with it and me.

I didn't know love, and I didn't know how to date or love someone who truly cared about me. All I knew were the casual friendships I obtained in school, and the various married couples in my family, but what was in between. This was more than friendship, but definitely not marriage, yet he cared so much. On father's day of 2005, I expressed my love to Derek the only way I knew how...sex. I laid on the floor in his bedroom while reading in the most seductive way I knew, but Derek ignored me. I had just given him a father's day card, so in my mind I for sure knew that he had sex plenty of times. I started to think that if he has a child, but isn't interested in having sex with me, that means he wasn't truly attracted to me. That night I did something that I never thought I would do...I begged him to have sex with me. I started an argument with Derek about his lack of attention even though I was trying my best to seduce him. He wanted to prove to me that wasn't his intentions, so he let his guard down and caved into my desire for passionate sex.

Since I was already on the floor, that's where we

started. I got a rug burn while riding, so he moved us to the bed to finish. I felt loved, but he felt guilty. I soon realized that he was very much so attracted to me and it came out when we had sex, but that's not how he wanted it to be.

College move-in day came fast and it was hard for us to part ways after spending so much time together over the summer. He was an Engineering major attending Delaware State University and I was a Pre-medicine major attending Elizabethtown College. Move-in night we left my parents in my dorm room to finish getting my room setup and went for a walk. My parents weren't comfortable, so we took my new roommate. Of course we ditched her along the way. We found a bathroom on the first floor of the dorm that seemed pretty secluded and went into the handicap stall. We started kissing and he unbuttoned my pants, turned me around, caressed my hips and bent me over. As he entered my ocean my legs got weak, but he held me up with his muscular grip as he stroked me from the back. I held onto the bathroom wall as my eyes rolled to the back of my head. When he finished, he pulled me up and kissed my neck as he held me and told me he loved me.

My freshmen year in college he gave me the best surprise. With my birthday being in October, there wasn't a lot of time from the start of the school year, but he somehow got my roommates phone number. Every morning my roommate would go for a run and tell me if "I'm not back in an hour come look for me". But that morning I heard my roommate re-enter their room faster than usual. I was still sleeping, but could always hear her come in. That morning was different though. I felt someone standing over me, so I forced my eyes open to find that it was Derek. After spending time together, he told me to get dressed and go check my mail in the student center. He kissed me and told me he would meet me over there shortly.

When I got to the mailroom, I found a box that read Pro Flowers. As I was opening the box, Derek entered the student center with a smile on his face. The box contained a dozen beautifully colored roses in a nice vase, a teddy bear, and some chocolate. I was ecstatic. We went back to my dorm room. My roommate wasn't there. He told me he wanted to give me my last birthday gift. He grabbed my hips and pulled me to him and slid one hand up to my breast as he place his full lips on my neck. As he kissed my neck and shoulders, he undressed me slowly. I climbed in my bed and laid on my back. I bit my lip while I waited for him to undress and join me. He opened my legs and placed himself between my thick thighs. He started passionately kissing my lips, and then his fingers entered my abyss to warm me up. He replaced his fingers with his erect thickness and began stroking. He bit his lip and whispered a moan "Fuck" as he sped up his stroke in bliss. We were so deep in the moment nothing else mattered. Until my roommate keyed in the room and caught us having sex. She told everyone on the floor and went and knocked on my RAs door. I didn't see the big deal. Her boyfriend came over every weekend when I went home and I'm sure they had lots of fun when I wasn't there.

Sex overtook our relationship. We were falling apart. I started feeling convicted because this was going against the Christian upbringing in which I was raised, and something about this relationship was different. I didn't want it to be like the others. But Derek's sex drive was more intense than ever. I began rejecting him, and he began wondering if I was cheating. Derek was trying to hold onto our relationship, but his desire for sex was a turn off for me. I never stopped to think that the day I begged for sex, was the day I determined the future of my relationship with Derek. My lack of sexual attention led him to start checking my phone and computer, until one day he found what he was looking for. An old childhood friend of mine left some messages on my AOL instant messenger that sent

Derek into an angry tantrum. That was the worst fight we ever had.

Our relationship grew from that night and withstood the tests of time through attending college in two different states, baby momma drama, court dates, family issues, etc. But the more our relationship grew, the more the sex grew. I was so worried about the sex that I missed the little things Derek did for me. Derek didn't want to lose me, so he continued to power through our relationship. We got better for a while and began mutually spoiling each other with time, gifts, affection, etc. Christmas of my sophomore year, Derek came to my school to celebrate the twelve days of Christmas with me before heading home for break. He showered me with gifts and love. He even brought me sexy lingerie to try to encourage the mood. I loved my new edition, but I did not want to have sex with Derek. We were doing so well. His intense sex drive made it hard to resist. He even turned on porn and told me to watch it to get in the mood. I watched it for a little while, but it wasn't working, my entire body felt numb and my surroundings were a blur. I had completely zoned out.

I was doing so well with his daughter, and he was so used to being a mature man, that he started thinking about the future with me. That wasn't a bad thing, but he was determined to have a son. And I was determined to finish the degree that I started.

That night while we were up hanging out, I had a craving for some ice cream, so at 2 a.m., Derek went to the grocery store and brought my favorite flavor. He read me a poem he had written on shipping paper from UPS and told me that he loved me. Then he looked at me and asked, "Why do you love me?" I hesitated, and zoned out. It felt like his face was a blur at that point. I told him that I love him and that should be enough. I had sex with him again, not because I wanted to, but because I felt bad. This was the first relationship that I had been in where a man gave to me just as much if not more that what I gave to him. But when Derek asked me why I loved him, I couldn't answer.

Looking back at this relationship, I realized Derek was far from a user; he actually was my first love. He didn't want to have sex with me, because he didn't want sex to ruin our relationship. He knew his body, and he knew how he felt about me. He tried to get me to see my worth, but I was too young to understand. Sex became the driver and our love started to take a backseat, but our friendship kept us on autopilot. We use to have a great relationship, and an even better friendship, but the addiction that I created was tearing us apart.

I tried breaking up with him, but I grew so attached to his daughter and I brought them both into my family's lives that it made the decision even harder. Every time I would try to break up with him, a holiday would come around and I didn't want him and his daughter to be without a loving atmosphere. I looked at him and saw the history we built, but I knew that I was battling a war within myself to change. He tried to attend church with me, but that wasn't his foundation. It took me so long to realize that he loved me, yet the damage was already done. I was too young to know how to fix it, but I knew I had to get out before I ended up pregnant.

The more distant I became, the more persistent he became. Valentine's Day was the next holiday to come. He planned a big date night for me. I'm sure he could feel something was up, but that was our last time together as a couple.

5

The Cougar

I took a gamble one summer and had a fling with a guy named Chance. He was young a sexy piece of eye candy. A football player at a local high school. I changed this young boy's life! I know what ya'll are thinking and the answer is yes...I did turn him out, in more ways than one.

Chance and I met while I was giving a group of High School students a tour of a local university's campus. Normally when I'm working I'm in my zone, but it was something about him that caught me eye. We had that immediate chemistry that neither one of us could hide. He was sexy! Thick, muscular build, chiseled, full pink lips, sharp cut, swag, height, and a voice that could make your knees go weak. It was the summer time, so the sunlight was shining on him just right as the sweat dripped down his face and ripped muscular arms, making his caramel complexion glisten. He was my Pretty Young Thing (PYT) I know what ya'll are thinking. Didn't you learn anything? Well yes I did. But obviously not enough yet. He smooth talked his way into getting my number, and that was the start of me and Chance's summer adventure.

That night we talked on the phone and he said all the right things. Typical of most first time conversations right? I pulled up to his house in my 2007 two-door silver cougar. It was pitch-black dark outside. He lived in the woods, no streetlights or civilization for that matter. I greeted him with a kiss and he drove. We were only meeting up for one thing...sex. We pulled up to an office building complex and parked. I had on a summer maxi. As he started kissing me, he ran his hand up my left thigh. As he reached my pussy and noticed that I already removed my panties, he pulled his head back slightly with a smirk on his face and whispered softly, "Easy access. Just the way I like it..."

I don't know what it was about his touch, but it was electrifying. My pussy started to twitch and I felt myself getting wet. My dress was going to be soaked because I didn't have on panties to catch my oceanic juices. He slipped two fingers inside my pussy and let the other massage my clit. I was now making whimpering noises as he kissed me. My heart was beating heavy, and my juices were flowing strong. All the sudden he stopped. I was lost. He got out of the car walked around the back to the passenger's side, opened my door and took my hand. He pulled me up out of the seat turned my backside towards the front of his pelvis and held me tight. He took two steps back with me in his arms as he closed the car door. Kissing on my neck and holding me with his right arm, he began moving his sweats out of the way so his erectness could make way for my oceanic abyss. He pulled my dress up above my hips, bent me over and entered my abyss.

Our summer adventure consisted of us meeting up just like that night. He would find a different place for us to explore, then we would mark our territory of memories outside on benches, my car, or whatever scenery we had around us.

As the summer came to an end, he wanted to see me one last time. By this time his car was fixed, so he came to me. He showed up at my dorm room one night looking like a snack. It was a grey sweatpants type of night. He spread my succulent thighs apart, climbed into the bed and slowly entered his body aligning his pelvis with mine. Something was different that night though. He wanted to cuddle and talk. He laid between my thighs fully clothed. He told me that he loved Big Beautiful Women (BBW), but the image of him being a star football player caused for him to date cheerleader type girls. We talked about everything that night from our strengths and weaknesses, to school, sports, hobbies and beyond. It was this relationship that I learned that love is not just sex and intimacy isn't always sexual. We fell asleep that night holding each other. That night he learned from me, and I learned from him.

6

One Night Stand (Nameless)

Most people think that a one night stand is the person you pick up at the bar and go home drunk with, only to wake up to fragmented memories. But what if I told you about a different type of one night stand? The kind where the man taps into your mind, passes through your heart, and knocks at the eternal entrance of your soul, only for it to end before you wake up the next day. This happened to me! He was still a random man; I met him on MySpace (common now, but not the smartest idea back in 2007). He was intrigued with getting to know me, and was excited to share his career goals, dreams, and desires with me. A working man with a great job and even bigger sense of community and family. So we decided to meet in person. Even though he worked a lot, he decided to come straight to my dorm after work (again probably not the smartest idea). I thought that being in a building full of students, I would be heard or helped if anything went wrong.

When he arrived, my confidence as a woman quickly withered to the insecurities of my past. I had so many thoughts running through my head, and instead of looking at him to see if he was my type, all I could think about is if I was his type. The wait as he walked from the parking lot to my building felt like an hour, but it was more like three minutes. A strong knock to my dorm door alerted me that it was happening…it was go time. I opened the door to a 6'2, mocha chocolate skinned, and muscular built man in a security uniform. As he passed through the doorway, I starred at him smiling. We got comfortable on the bed and started talking, since there was nowhere else to sit. As he starred at me, I asked him if I was as pretty as he said I was in my pictures. I kept removing my glasses, knowing that my sparkling brown eyes were the main attraction of my mocha chocolate facial features. He affirmed my beauty with a strong yes and a kiss to my forehead. My head got so big! I forgot everything we just talked about, the only thing that mattered was keeping him, and I thought for sure at that hour, he was there for one thing. Well yes, me of course...but ALL of me! Because surely my intellect and beauty were not enough to keep a more mature man's attention, especially after hours (or so I thought). So I started to move my body to the beat of the music playing softly in the background from my computer on the desk. I adjusted my eyes and batted them just enough for them to grab his attention so he could look deep. I advanced with a kiss and rolled over so that I sat straddled on top of him, gazing into the dark rounds of his pupils. The conversations became phrases, those phrases became seductive foreplay, and the foreplay turned into sex.

There I was once again on my back, looking into the face of a man I thought would dive into my internal ocean and find love between my thighs. With my hormones raging and my ocean flowing, he asked if I was ready, I replied yes. I opened my thick, succulent thighs as he guided himself into my extremely wet pussy. As his dick hit the walls of my vagina, the guilt hit my soul, but the feeling hit my flesh and I continued to let him stroke. In intimacy, I realized I felt different physically...it started hurting. So I quickly asked him to pull out. I got on top thinking it would make it better, and it did physically, but it only felt worse on my internal. I told him I couldn't do it and climbed off. Sitting next to him on my bed he chuckled and told me he knew I wasn't ready. I tensed up thinking he was mad at me. He looked at me and said you wanted this, not me, but I'm a man so I wasn't going to say no. Relax! We talked for the rest of the night until we both fell asleep.

He woke up the next morning and kissed me on my cheek before proceeding to leave. I looked at the clock and realized that I was late for the Annual AIDS walk in downtown Wilmington that my student organization at college participated in every year. I wanted him to stay, but we both had things to do. I watched his back as the door closed behind him. A thought came to mind just as the door latched…I never caught his name. I only knew what they called him on MySpace. All of this happened within a span of 24 hours. I always heard of a one night stand, but I just made one my reality. And just like that as short as this chapter is it was over. MySpace connections were deleted along with a piece of me. That sad part is, I was sober.

7
Toxic Times

First of all, the red flag should have come when we crossed paths in a police station. I was there getting finger printed since I worked with kids, so I thought maybe he could be there doing something similar. Ha! I laugh at my naiveté now. He was slick and got my number from a form I filled out and called me that night. After hanging up on him a few times, he was finally able to spark conversation with me. Needless to say, we talked until the sun came up the next day.

He wanted to meet up. The first place I went to visit him was a first floor studio apartment in some run down building that wasn't even his apartment. Another red flag was thrown, but my kind heart (or stupid mind) looked past the reality of what was, and looked at it as humble beginnings of what could be. We enter the small, dimly lit efficiency and proceeded to the back where a mattress laid on the floor of the kitchen. Of course I was hesitant to even sit down, but something was interrupting my logical thinking. Everything I was ever taught went out the window.

I took classes that summer, so I had him come back to the dorms. Of course there was nowhere to sit and relax except for the small twin XL bed. He kicked off his shoes to climb onto the bed and I noticed a pungent smell hit my nose…it was his feet. I gasped and held my breath, trying not to noticeably cover my nose. I guess he noticed it too because he excused himself to the bathroom and I heard my shower turn on. When he returned we could finally focus on each other instead of that hideous smell. He wanted to taste my juices. So he made his requests known verbally then executed physically. As long as his feet weren't near me I was cool.

A couple weeks later he moved from the efficiency with some of his boys near 4th and Monroe Street. The house was really nice, but that probably wasn't the best area for me to start hanging out. I spent the night there one night. We ordered food from Pete's Pizza, watched a movie, and talked. It was cool. It was the one time he paid for the food...or anything for that matter since we were together. It seemed like it pained him to give his card number over the phone for the little $25 of food we ordered. In my head I was thinking that's nothing compared to all the money I've spent on gas, food, etc.

He told me to sleep on the couch and he made a palette on the floor. As soon as I dozed off, several gunshots fired from outside the window. It sounded way to close for comfort and left a ringing in my ears. I didn't grow up in that type of environment so I was scared. I jumped off the couch onto the floor where he was. He laughed and said

"What are you doing?"

I said, "You didn't hear that?"

He said, "Yea, but it's not enough room for you and me to sleep down here so get back on the couch!"

In my head I was thinking are you serious? There is someone shooting on the corner of the block and the house we are in is a corner unit. I was pissed, disappointed, and trembling in fear. I just kept looking at the almost floor to ceiling window thinking a stray bullet could hit me because I was the one sitting up higher. It seemed like he didn't care and I couldn't just walk outside and get into my car and go.

It was back to school for the fall semester, so we went to Target on 202 to grab some stuff for my dorm. We stopped by the house on Munroe before returning to campus. I don't know what was going on that night, but when we came out, the entire street was blocked off and cops were everywhere. I knew I couldn't back up the street because that would draw attention to my car. He kept telling me he couldn't encounter the police, but I told him to chill and let me handle everything. I inched up to the checkpoint and two cops approached my car...one on each side. I rolled my window down and presented the officer with my license and registration. He peeped the F.O.P. sign on my car, which sparked conversation. I let out a deep exhale thinking that we were in the clear. But then, this dude made the dumbest move ever. I don't know why he always wore grey sweatpants with loose change in his pockets. He was tall and my two-door sports car wasn't the best for his legroom. Right as the officers went to walk away, he put his legs down causing all the change to hit the sides of the car interior. The noise sparked the cops' attention and they immediately turned towards the car. The next thing I knew I was on the ground with my face in the dirty cement trying to figure out what the heck just happened.

I don't know why I didn't move on after all of this. My next move was the unthinkable. I let him move in with me. Yes…at school. He was drunk, and I was there, so that night my worst fear became my reality. This is the one time I was hoping a student would hear the shatters of my belongings hitting the floor; my feminine screams for help, and tussle of two bodies and call the police, but nobody came. I was stuck. My back thrown into the cement cylinder walls of the tiny dorm room. He reached for both of my arms and pulled them together tightly, putting both of my wrists together. I begged him to stop, but he was drunk and angry.

"We fucked before and now you don't want me?" he yelled. "Huh? Answer me…you don't want me? Well you don't have a choice tonight."

My body became a ping-pong ball bouncing off the walls and objects around the room as he thrusts me around ripping my clothes off and grabbing my body parts. I was naked and afraid. He had a look in his eyes that I never saw before. I decided I better follow his directions, but that wasn't good enough for him. I wasn't moving quickly enough. Begging him to calm down was only making things worse. He tossed me on the bed. I turned around quickly. He grabbed me tightly.

"Where are you going?" he yelled! "I told you the deal!"

He grabbed my legs and pulled me down on the bed so my back was flat. Spreading my thick thighs apart, he put my legs on his shoulders, lowered himself to me and brutally thrusts his dick into my vagina. His strokes were powerful. I was fighting back tears and trying to position my head so that I did not have to look at him. Each stroke felt like a lifetime before it would end. He sped up and pulled out leaving his cum all over me. He rolled over to the side of me as I slid from underneath him. As he dozed off I slipped out of the bed.

I found a spot to sleep on the cold, hard, tile floor of my dorm room as a cried silently to myself. Through the blurs of my tears I looked at the broken items around my room, and as I moved I felt the pain of my sore muscles. The room was pitch black, but the street light from outside shined through the crack of my broken blinds. I looked at my wrists and they were red and swollen. I had bruises from the tugging and rough squeezing. He was not gentle at all that night. He was brutal...physically and emotionally. Although I was in a sunken place, I prayed to God that night and asked him to forgive me of my sins before I took a deep breath and closed my eyes to sleep.

The next morning he woke up, looked around the room and sat up on the bed. I was still on the floor...awake, but positioned as if I was still sleeping.

"Tiphane!" he yelled. "What happened in here?"

I was nervous to respond, so I laid there quietly trying to collect my words. I wasn't sure what to say, but I knew he had to go. I sat up slowly squinting my face and eyes as I endured the pain of my soreness.

"You got drunk" I replied softly. "And messed up my room last night...and...and you hurt me."

Of course he denied it. He started yelling at me. Could you believe this dude? He is in my room that I pay for yelling at me after he just took everything from me. Ha! Well guess what? I only needed that one time. I stood up with the strength I had and told him to take his one bag and get out. He chuckled and said he was meeting a girl on Main Street anyway. For a minute I was hurt when he said he was treating her to breakfast thinking about all that I had done for him, but then I snapped out of it. He had to go! He didn't go out without an argument though. After a while, I opened my door and forced him out...it was leave or get escorted out by the police. He couldn't afford another encounter with the police. That was the last I saw him.

From that one encounter that night, I lost it all. My

job, my housing, my GPA for the semester, but more importantly...myself. I had lost myself somewhere along the way in this relationship, and I was so deep in that it cost me everything except my physical life. How could I have allowed this to happen, but more importantly, how was I going to explain this to my parents?

8

Heartbreak

Pusher Girl…a name once called by him, but I felt more like a push over by the time all was said and done. Slowly erasing memories is all that I have left…a fading image of what I pictured my life to be…the ignorance, carelessness, every man is the same internally with a different shell…life's lessons accompanied by heartache and tears. We communicated through poetry in our beginning stages of bliss. He called me his addiction. His Pusher Girl. Dealing love to him and pushing it deep into his blood stream, becoming hooked on the medicine of cloud nine. One of mine was *Look, Listen and Learn.*

Look, listen and learn,

A message that truly burns,

Burns deep in my soul to release,

Release a secret that I can no longer keep,

Keep deep within my tunnel,

Tunnel of emotions that went away when I look,

Look deep into your fiery eyes,

Eyes filled with heated passion,

Passion of love that flares,

Flares and then coasts...

Coasts into beautiful galaxies,

Galaxies that sparkle,

Sparkly back at me as I gaze,

Gaze deep,

Deep into the twinkling stars of your pupils a connection full of heat.

And then it starts,

Starts to speed up,

Up like a virtual video game,

Game that has me in a total twilight zone,

Zone free and in his arms...tight,

Tight and held is where I want to be,

Be for eternity,

Eternity of laughter, love and passion that never fades.

And then I stopped...

Stopped to listen,

Listen to the uncontrollable beats,

Beats that I learned were my heartbeat,

My heart beat like a car speeding on the freeway.

And then we merged,

Merged his lips into mine,

Mine soft, his full, now our tongues were intertwined,

Intertwined desirable feelings arousing from within,

Within the butterflies of my stomach and then…

A dead moment,

Moment filled with anxiousness,

Anxiousness to know the next move,

Move closer to him and me to him as his thickness peaks,

Peaks and then leans in closer to whisper as he speaks,

Speaks words that I've heard before – I got you and you got me.

Me? I replied as he moves my hands to his chest…I sighed,

Sighed in relief to know his heart also beats an indescribable speed.

So what to do now?

Now that we both know our true feelings,

Feelings that I'm not sure if lust or love…the PRESSURE

Pressure of uncertainty,

Uncertainty of the outcome of this,

This lesson I have just taught,

Taught him about my feelings...or maybe myself to distinguish lust and love.

Did I just learn?

Learn that the one I have just looked at and listened to is the one my heart, mind and soul yields to?

We grew up together as friends. Most people say marry your best friend. Others say never date your friend, you'll ruin your friendship. I went the route of thinking I would marry my best friend, but little did I know I was a friend of convenience.

Lamar was a military man. He signed up straight out of high school. We were close until I lost touch with him after his first deployment to Iraq. One day, I received a call from a weird number. It generated from overseas. It was the hospital in Iraq letting me know that his platoon had gotten blown up in the field. I was on his emergency contact list and the only one who picked up. I didn't know what to do. I was frantic. I couldn't believe this was happening, but I was glad that he was still alive. From that day on we became closer than ever. I was sending him care packages and checking on him the best I could until he returned to the base in California. When he got back, he called me and made "us" official. My caring for him the past couple months made him reflect on how close we always were, the fact that life is too short, and I'm an amazing woman.

For my birthday in October 2007, I decided to fly out to California where he was stationed. I didn't realize that flights to California were so expensive, but I put it on my credit card. I was in college, and I had already made poor choices with it, so why not? When I arrived at the airport he was waiting outside in his brand new dodge avenger with tinted windows all around and an extended custom package. As I walked out the door with my sunglasses on and wind blowing through my jet black, fresh press and curled hair, he smiled from ear to ear and made his way over to me to greet me with a kiss. He was fully clothed in his marine camos since he was on duty, so we didn't have much time. We got back to the base where he took me to the barracks so I could take a nap. It didn't look or feel much different than my dorm room, so I was cool.

As I was sleeping, I heard the door creak. He came back on his break to check on me. I felt his full soft lips kiss my forehead and my body quivered as his gentle touch ran his hands up the left side of my curves to pull the blankets up. He left a note for me next to the bed that I found when I woke up. I couldn't wait for him to get off work and neither could he. I was all he could think about, and the note had me smiling from ear to ear. You already know what that means. Oh yea…it definitely got heated. Standing over top of the bed, he wrapped him arms around my thick thighs and turned my body around so my legs were off the bed just enough to wrap around his pelvis. He was stronger than he looked in stature…Marine strong! He slowly slid his masculine hands up the curves of my body and stopped at my cantaloupe breasts to give them a firm squeeze before bending over to give me a kiss. He began to explore my body with his mouth, giving special attention to some areas with his tongue.

"I want to taste you." He whispered in the moment.

He began unbuckling my pants and sliding them down my hips. I had to help him because that was a lot of meat to get my tight jeans over without interrupting the moment. He gently spread my legs and placed his head between them. As I felt the tip of his nose rub against my lips and clitoris, I quivered. As his fingeres plunged into my abyss followed by his thick tongue, I moaned deeply. My ocean was flowing, but he was the human cup at the end to catch every drop. After he got me aroused and engaged, he stood up, gazing into my eyes with his hypnotic bedroom eyes. He continues to massage my clit with one hand as he let his pants down with the other. Staring into each other's eyes, he inched his fully erect dick into my pussy. It had been a while, but I trusted him. I moaned deeply as my heart rate increased while I closed my eyes to enjoy the moment of bliss.

After we got done he sprung it on me that I couldn't stay in the barracks. I wasn't use to military life, so I didn't know I would have to find my own place to stay. I thought that he could get a hotel or somewhere for me to stay on base. He drove me to a hotel nearby. It was nice, but it was California so of course it wasn't cheap. He didn't have the money to help, so it was all on me. I was already out there so what could I do. He stayed with me at the hotel each night, but he had to work on base most of the time I was there during the day. Since I didn't have a car, it wasn't much sightseeing I could do during the day. But I was always into something, so I had plenty of work with me to occupy my time. We spent lots of time together in the evenings when he got off work. Attending the movies, shopping at the mall, eating sushi and some other hot spots in California he wanted me to see. It was an awesome time, except...I paid for it all. For both of us. It was my birthday, but I was swiping my credit card like I just hit the lottery. I even bought him a $200 custom batman and joker racecar jacket. That's back when the M&M and other race car jackets were the thing.

I spent five days in California and left on early in the morning on the sixth day. He didn't want me to leave just as much as I didn't want to leave. He spoke about the future and coming back to Delaware so we could start our life together once they discharged him from the military. I tried to delay my flight, but I was already broke, so I had to go. The tight goodbye hug was hard to bear. I walked towards the door of the airport, to the check-in counter, and eventually on the escalator to the TSA line, looking back sparingly until I could no longer see his car in sight.

The holidays were coming and I wanted him to see his family. He hadn't seen them since he was sent back the U.S. from the hospital in Iraq. He told me they were not paying him until the end of December. Christmas was big in my family and I felt bad that he wouldn't be able to come home to see his. So, I whipped out my credit card and paid for the $600 flight for him to come home.

Lamar had a best-friend named Memphis. His girlfriend and I got cool, so we decided to link up for New Year's Eve. Diamond and Memphis had traditions in their relationship, like a midnight kiss every New Year's Eve no matter where they are. But she was also raised in the church, and her dad was a pastor, so she wanted to go to church first. Diamond and I attended her father's church for New Year's Eve service. It was good vibes and a great time. We left around 11:45 p.m. so we could make it to Memphis' house for the big midnight kiss. We drove separate cars, so I followed her. Speeding down 273, I was just as excited for her to fulfill her fantasy kiss. When we pulled up to the house, I noticed a hesitation from her and I did not see anyone coming out of the house. He stood her up. She was furious. I felt bad so I invited her to hang out with Lamar and me at his cousin's house gathering to ring in the New Year...BIG MISTAKE. Hurt people really do hurt people even if it's unintentional.

When we walked in Lamar's eyes read, "What happened? What is she doing here?" I didn't want to get into what happened because I knew she was crushed, so everyone welcomed her with open arms and started mingling. Lamar made Mimosas and served his mix of drinks. I wasn't drinking that night, but everyone else in the room was. Diamond started getting loose. She removed her coat. Her coat slowly slid off her shoulders to reveal her petite stature in an all black, spandex dress hugging her curves in all the right places. Her skin was glowing in a caramel bronze complexion and her hair; light brown, pressed with pin curls that moved loosely with each head turn. She wore it for Memphis, but since he stood her up, everyone got the pleasure of it that night. The drinks got her lose, and she began to flirt…with my boyfriend.

As the clock struck midnight everyone was drunk but me. All the jokes were funny to those intoxicated, and our welcomed yet unwelcomed guest was nestled under my boyfriend in bliss. I wanted to be with him, but my phone was messing up so I couldn't even text him. I didn't know what to do to lure him out of the room without causing a jealous scene and all eyes turning on me as the party pooper.

Lamar carried her to her car, placed her in the passenger seat and slammed the door. He walked around to the driver's side, got in and started the car. I followed behind him in my car. Lamar was finally able to get a hold of Memphis. He took her in the house to him. He returned to the car and got in the passengers seat since I was the designated driver for the night. We rode to his grandmother's house in silence. Except for the one sentence when he told me he knew something was bothering me. When we got to the house, he stripped down to his boxers, climbed in the bed and went to sleep.

"There I was, 20 years old bringing in the New Year

crying myself to sleep next to the man I thought was the man of my dreams. The way our relationship formed was like a fantasy on TV. Every touch was like cloud nine. But when I think about all the things I have done for him, I can't believe he can lay there sleeping, listening to my cries and not care.

I know this dude hears me, but he wasn't going to wake up to tend to my hurting heart. So I wiped my tears and climbed into the bed. Staring at the window as the streetlight peeped through the cracks of the blinds. I zoned out until I fell asleep.

The next morning, Lamar opened up to me. He said he heard me crying, but he didn't feel like dealing with me so he went to sleep. He didn't have many words for me. He grabbed my shirt and pulled me to his dark chocolate skin. As he starred into my brown eyes, he bit his bottom lip. He put his forehead to mine and led in to give me a gentle kiss on my lips. He made passionate love (well, lust) to me that morning. When we finished he said, "There...Happy New Year. You got what you wanted."

After the whole New Year's situation, Lamar became distant. The night before his flight back home, he decided to tell me that he no longer wanted to move to Delaware. There was nothing there for him. I was crushed. We planned out everything. He was getting out of the military on honorable discharge and I was almost finished my Bachelors at University of Delaware. His mom had moved to Colorado, so we were supposed to live in her house in Delaware to start off. We had it all planned out, but he didn't want it...didn't want me. I was crushed. But I didn't know that in the days to come I would be even more heartbroken.

When he returned home, I learned of a girl through MySpace from North Carolina that he had been talking to. He moved her to California the month he left me and they started a life together. He said she needed him. He flew her to California, got an apartment and they moved in together.

9

Life Intermission

AAAAAAHHHHHHHHH!!!!!!! I wish I could scream through this page so you could hear my anger! After everything I went through! How could he do this to me? I trusted him! I was giving my all to these men from the inside out. And for what? NOTHING! My credit cards were backed up from buying love. I was in debt from putting love on credit thinking that one day it would pay me back. I recognized that I was a giver, but I was overcompensating in my love language to these men. This was frustrating, hurtful, annoying...I blamed myself. Receiving gifts wasn't my love language, but I thought my effort and thoughtfulness would be the perfect gesture of love.

I was done with relationships after it didn't work out with Lamar. They say karma has a way of handling those who have wronged us, and in this case that came true. I found out that the girl played Lamar from North Carolina not too long after he moved her out there. Listening to the story was crazy because it was literally play-by-play of our relationship. He gave to her the same way I gave to him. Paid for her flight out there, took her shopping, pleased her and loved her. All for her to give him a thank you...if that and go about her way. I can't say I was happy. I never want anyone to experience the heartbreak I felt. All I could think was "Wow that's crazy."

After being raped and being hurt by the person who was one of my best friends, I couldn't take it. I felt like I was pouring so much into other people with nothing in return. Who was I going to talk to about all of these relationships without feeling like a hoe? It was me and my darkness once again, left to sort through the woes of life.

10

I Was the Side Chick and Didn't Know It

I wasn't given the opportunity to let go....I was forced to let go and there is definitely a big difference....I can't even say he moved on fast, because the other chick never left. She was always there, she was his main love. I was so stuck with confusion and hurt that it put me in a depressed state of mind. To give your ALL and then having to let go because they were never going to give you their heart, hurt like hell. I wasn't even able to get a chance to fix it. He really had me believing that I was all that he wanted, but he left me in a dust of memories like I was nothing. I had no choice but to let go. I thought he was coming along to make me happy again. I was always willing to take a risk on love. To keep my mind and heart open in hopes that one day it would be the final one, but this wasn't it.

We met through a mutual friend of mine at college. She was a lot older than me. You know...the ones that graduate, but still hang around and live in the off campus houses so you think they are still a student...yea that was her. She was very friendly and I was young and naïve. I never knew that a woman could play you just as much as a man. She was a manipulator...a good one at that. Her name was Yolanda. She was in a sorority and dated a guy in Texas in a fraternity. I got cool with her boyfriend Tyson by phone because I was around her a lot. It was him that introduced me to Rob. We immediately vibed. I wasn't looking for a relationship though. I mean I had already been through hell. But he had ulterior motives. Our conversations went from friendly to freaky very quickly. He was a typical guy. His visual nature for feminine body parts was apparent when he quickly pointed out my 38DDs in a headshot he saw of me. Since the four of us seemed to vibe well, Yolanda suggested the guys come to Delaware during Rob's Spring Break. I would still be in classes, but I didn't mind because Yolanda has a house off campus and volunteered to host the guys there.

After we planned it all out, Yolanda told me that she had some money coming in, but it hadn't hit her account yet, so she asked me to pay for Rob and Tyson's flights. She said that Rob had never flown before and both of them were scared of airplanes and wouldn't fly without the other. I really wanted to see Rob, so I agreed to pay, thinking that I would be paid back. I used my good old credit card once again and paid for two flights from Texas to Philadelphia.

The days leading up to their arrival seemed like forever. Rob was enticed with me. As a talker, I was always open to new conversation and new people, but I can't say I was as into him. We grew closer the more he talked. It's like we lived on the phone together...even when he was at work. I never knew that someone else was in the picture because it seemed like the only thing he had time for and made time for was me. Silly me! When you can't physically see someone you really don't know what they are doing because there are always times when they don't talk to you. As you will see in the matter of days we went from bliss to blah.

Day 1 – The day before the guys arrived, Yolanda told me that something came up with her house and the boys couldn't stay with her for the entire week. One thing I was good at was connects, so I called my Marriott connect. I really do have some great friends. My girl Camille drove to Delaware from PG County Maryland the day the guys were arriving to check me into the hotel. Shout out to the $25 per night rate that I received! University of Delaware (UD) had a Marriott right on campus, so it was perfect. The guys weren't flying in till that night, so I checked the room and went about the rest of my day.

Later that night I grabbed my girl Amber to ride with me to get the boys. Anyone who knows me knows that I can't see that well at night so I needed a rollie. We parked in the garage and walked to the baggage claim for Southwest Airlines. Rob knew what I was wearing, but I had no idea what they would have on. As he came down the escalator, Rob and I immediately connected eyes. The only thing I could think though was "Man is Tyson short. He and Yolanda make a weird couple." I quickly put my attention back on Rob.

When we got back to the room, Rob didn't waste any time. As soon as our bags hit the floor he whispered in my ear,

"I wasn't playing. I'm about to do every thing to you I ever told you over the phone."

He didn't even care that Tyson was in the room. Guys

already know the deal though, so Tyson left the room. I was very hesitant at first because I was just meeting him. I don't know what's up with me and sex, but it seemed like that's all there was to give in order to be with them.

Rob was too excited to see my cantaloupes in person. He slid his hands up my shirt and gripped them firmly as he leaned in for a kiss. He had very full, pink lips. He knew he was getting some that night. He groped every part of my body with his masculine touch to get me aroused and kissed every potential spot he could think of me to have. It worked, he was turning me on. And as much as I wanted him to stop, my flesh wanted his heat to continue to spark mine.

Tyson had perfect timing…he came back to the room right as we finished. Before we dozed off, Rob realized that he left his wallet at home.

Day 2 – The next morning I called Yolanda. Somehow she got stuck at her parents' house in Maryland, so I was stuck with the guys. I was pissed! I mean it's not like you forgotten they were here. You planned this trip with me. I ordered the guys pizza and decided to get out of the room. We got on the UD shuttle and went to Trabant Student Center. While we were sitting in the food court, my girl Daisy walked in. I left the guys at the table and walked over to "the booth" where she was. Daisy was cool, but most men only saw her for her bubble butt. Of course the guys wanted to know who she was and told me to bring her over. She ended up coming back to the hotel with us to chill. After we made a stop at the liquor store to get the boys some beers. With Yolanda missing in action and Rob leaving his wallet in Texas, of course I paid for that too.

When we got back to the hotel, the guys started drinking and having a good time. We put on some music and they taught Daisy and I some southern dance moves. That turned into a pillow fight, which turned into wrestling. I noticed Rob was into Daisy, but I did my best to ignore it. In the midst of having a good time, Yolanda called and said her parents cooked us dinner and asked us to come get her…in Maryland…two hours away.

Day 3 – We linked up with Yolanda's sorority sister Stacy that was in a graduate program at University of Delaware and lived close to campus. Yolanda has a bright idea to do a dinner night for the guys and fellowship since the week wasn't going anywhere near as planned. When we got to the grocery store, Yolanda wanted to take the lead on the menu and food. I just let her live because I was over her at this point. My girls Amber and Destiny came along for the shenanigans to keep me sane. The food was nasty, but the time spent was cool, especially since my girls were there. The guys stayed at Stacy's apartment that night. Since she was Greek she didn't mind looking out for traveling fam. I headed to my parent's for a break.

Day 4 – I was tired of being in Delaware doing nothing after spending so much money to fly Rob out here, so I hit up my friend Camille to see what she was doing. She lived right near a metro stop not too far from FedEx stadium. I told Rob I was taking him to D.C. and left Tyson to Yolanda since he was her responsibility. The drive to D.C. was dope. Singing old school songs, talking and vibing...more than anything, I thought Rob was a great friend. Camille was from the south, so I knew the hospitality would be on point when we got to her house. She has a 2-year-old son who Rob interacted great with. We decided to go explore some of the free museums in D.C. since Rob had never been to the east coast. We stayed the night at Camille's and headed back to Delaware the next morning.

Day 5 – On his last day he was very distant. I knew something happened back home. I just didn't know what. I found him sitting in the pool area of the Marriott Hotel where we stayed looking down. I walked in and sat next to him, hoping to comfort whatever the need was. He was ready to go home and nothing I could do or was doing would help. Rob and I hung out at Daisy's house until it was time to go back to the airport. Yolanda wanted to spend some alone time with Tyson, so since she and Daisy lived on the same street we stayed there. Rob took a nap while Yolanda and I caught up on life.

We left out for the airport around 3am. Yolanda rode with me this time, so it was just the four of us. The goodbyes were bittersweet because I was confused from the shift in Rob's personality. On the ride back home all I could think about is what happened. Did someone in his family pass away? Was he upset with a family member? I wasn't sure, but after all I did to make sure they had a good time, I was disappointed in how it ended.

When he landed in Texas he called to thank me again for showing him a good time. He told me there was more that he wanted to say.

"Tiphane, I just want you to know that I have a girlfriend. We have been dating since we were fourteen years old and we are going to get married soon. I didn't mean to hurt you. I just was curious. And then I found you. I appreciate you showing me what real love is, so I can now show her the love she deserves. In that short time you showed me a lot."

The crazy thing is, this time I wasn't just played by a guy, I was played by a woman as well. Double used like I was a toy. I knew long distance relationships were a gamble, but I was young and willing to explore what was out there. I know I had been played in the past, but I definitely didn't see that coming. I wondered what lie he told his girlfriend to spend a week in little old Delaware. There were a lot of things that didn't make sense. And to be honest as much as I was angry, I was numb to hurt and just wanted to wake up from this dream so I didn't have to deal with it anymore.

Self Talk

This was the start of my eating disorder. I wanted so much to be like the other women I saw, but the pain I endured led me to cope through food. I didn't care about this part of my life. Every other area of my life excelled except relationships.

Today I see why I am worth the wait. It is more than finding "the one"; it is about building greatness and not settling for something fake. I no longer want to look at my age and wonder where my king is. I no longer want to look to my right or my left to see how other women live. I just want to live my life according to how God says. Not settling, and learning how to say NO. I want a best friend in my mate, not just for the first 5-10 years, but the full eternal life here on earth together. I want him to serve God with and without me. Someone that when the pastor says grab someone for a praise break, when I grab him, he got me. I want a man I can be me in the natural, but can turn up with in the spiritual. Where was I going wrong?

11

Life Intermission

A t this stage in my life it hit me...the need to change, the need for something different, something refreshing. I knew it was getting bad when I started living and acting out the hurt people hurt other people concept. I had been played and hurt so much, that I learned how to do it. I still had the charm that pulled these dudes, but I had the mindset of all their personalities...the abuser, the user, the womanizer, the sex addict...I remember playing this guy from Philly real good, or so I thought because the joke ultimately ended up being back on me. My crush from my freshman year of college wiggled his way back into my life. I had been there done that at this point and I wasn't going back! But the anger in me wanted revenge even if it wasn't the men that hurt me, so I used him. He was willing to give me money, trips, long talks…whatever I wanted. I milked it for a while, but the inner me wasn't really the player type, so I cut ties with him quickly.

I enrolled myself in Tiphane` University, a self-image healing clinic…a journey led by me for me to rid myself of the toxic impurities that plagued my mind, body, and soul. Self-love is important. An essential key in order for you to be your best self. I needed it. I was emotionally torn, physically eating myself to a heart attack, trying to throw it all back up to fit the image of the Victoria Secret models I thought I needed to become, while dealing with depression. Often we pour ourselves into someone else forgetting about the most important person, YOU. Love yours, but do not forget to love yourself. I realized this time that I had to heal on another level. My journey to self-image healing was a five-year stretch. I decided to choose myself for the first time in a long time. Before, I was putting all my effort into my relationships, but I was neglecting to fix the one I had with myself. A lot of times we don't love ourselves as much as we think we do & the relationships that we have with others brings that to the forefront. It was time to take care of me. I decided to grow myself in personal development, friendship/recreation, business, education, physical health and spirituality.

Personal Development

There are so many approaches to personal development. YouTube videos, audios, physical books, worship music, counseling...it really depends on your personality. For me, I was always into reading and writing, so I built my personal development around that. Most of the time I didn't want to read. I cried as I read. Sometimes I even throw the books across the room, dropped to my knees and screamed with tears flowing from my eyes. I knew I needed it though. I needed something to prevent me from going too far astray because I knew that I wouldn't come back.

Some of the books that helped me along the way were:

- *Boundaries in Dating: How Healthy Choices Grow Healthy Relationships* by Henry Cloud
- *Why Do Men Date Bitches?* by Sherry Argov
- *Why Do Men Marry Bitches?* by Sherry Argov
- *Women Thou Art Loose Women's Devotional Bible*

Friendship/Recreation

Our friends are big contributors to our circle, keeping

us on the right path, talking us off the ledge and reminding us of how amazing we are. Friendship was one of the main things that kept my mind from wandering and kept me in good spirits. God sent the right people in my path at the right time to enjoy life with in during this season of hurt. I spend my time eating at new restaurants, visiting new cities (I spent a lot of time in NYC), attending concerts, Broadway productions, and so many other events. My plate was just as full in my personal life as it was in business. It was just the balance I needed.

Journal Entry from August 21, 2011 "Today I woke up to receive a blessing of $800 from a great person who believes in my visions and ability to be successful. It's great to have friends that care enough to help you not just through thick and thin, but sponsor you to get to your end goal and win. At noon I got in the car with Jared A. Fletcher, a friend from college and made my way to New York City, one of our favorite spots to visit. It's funny because so many people say that Jared and I should date, but I cherish the friendship and the times that we share. We talk about everything and I am able to share how I really feel about life. The ride down was cool, we checked into the Marriott at the Newark, NJ Airport, took a quick nap, changed our clothes and went on our way. We parked at the mall to catch the train into the city. We took a taxi to the ferry and everything was cool until it started raining. The concert said rain or shine, so we got in the line and made our way to the ferry by now swaying in the wind as the storm viciously approaches. Once we docked in Governors Island, we proceeded to the concert and got in line only to be notified five minutes later that the event was canceled. By now it was raining cats and dogs, and the workers claimed that the next ferry was not leaving for while. As the crowd began to head back to the ferry to get out of this crazy weather, we began walking together under a small umbrella interlocked as quickly as we could so we did not miss the boat. Luckily we found seats and rested soaked in the evidence of Mother Nature. The ride back on the ferry was terrible because of the weather, but we made it back safe. When we exited the ferry, we put up our small umbrella and interlocked again...his hand around my shoulders and my hand on his waist walking down the city streets of NYC not really knowing where we were going and trying to find a taxi that was available in the chaos. After several full taxis and off the clock drive-byes as if we weren't there, we found a taxi to give a ride back to 42nd and Broadway. We walked to find me a pair of sneakers first since my genius self wore flip-flops. First to Champs in Times Square and then to Footlocker where I secured a pair, so now we could eat...B.B. kings it was. After the food gave us both cramps, we made the long walk back to the subway at the 33rd St station. From there we slept on each other for the train ride back to the car. Off the train we went through the mall to the parking garage only to find that our parking ticket was unreadable and it was after hours so pushing the button for help was of no assistance. There we stood...tired, crampy and now stuck in this garage in Jersey City. My magic touch fingers finally got the card to read so we could pay, so off we went...or so we thought. When we put the ticket in the machine to get out...it read unreadable at least 20 times and by then our 15 minute grace period was over, so I told Jared to piggy-back off someone to get us out of the garage...thank God that worked. We were finally free...besides driving up few ramps the wrong way trying to make our way back to the hotel, our night was smooth sailing after that:) Now that I am done writing this story I am signing off until next time. I love living vicariously with great friends."

I never realized the great group of people around me until this season of my life. Jared gave me hope again. He helped me realize how important friendship is. We were connected platonically. It was a great feeling to be open and carefree with a genuine individual. We were far from each other's type, so there were never any boundaries crossed in all the times we hung out together. Between him, my mom and the women God was sending in my life, friendship carried my through my dark times.

Business

My gifts truly made room for me during this season of my life. I was over church, people, and honestly life at this point. My brother was always my biggest fan though, so he was always plugging me to people. After months of being persistent, I started going to his church in 2009.

In 2010, my passion for women suffering in silence grew. After a long talk with my mom who encouraged me to go after any vision God set in my heart, I founded True Women of Virtue, LLC. The nonprofit was founded as a sisterhood for women to motivate, educate, and encourage entrepreneurship, redefine beauty, build new networks, and reassert a sense of assurance among women.

The more I followed my dreams, the more opportunities that were presented to me. Shortly after launching True Women of Virtue, I was asked to manage a singing group/band that later landed a record deal. From that opportunity, so I expanded my business to incorporate True Vision Management.

From these opportunities, my portfolio of entrepreneurship grew. In 2011, True Women of Virtue was awarded Business of the Year from the Delmarva Chapter of the Home-Based Business Chamber of Commerce and was nominated Best Female Business for the Delaware Black Business Awards.

Education

A year after my last break up, I graduated with my Bachelors of Arts from the University of Delaware and was asked to serve as the speaker for the Black American Studies commencement ceremony as the President of the Black Student Union.

Although I graduated with various awards and acknowledgements, I was so distracted with getting my life back on track my senior year that I neglected to prepare for the after life. I was determined to enroll in a Masters of Business Education program. With the help of my senior capstone professor, prayer and hard work, I was able to start my Masters immediately after graduating.

Health

The way I coped with the breakups I experienced was eating, but due to the loss of my aunt, and the humiliating way we were forced to funeralize her because of her weight, I knew that I couldn't continue on this road. I decided to get help.

I hated working out with men. It gave me anxiety. I remember hiding in locker rooms at times to avoid the big cardio rooms full of women half dressed and men who pretend to lift heavy weights to flirt with these women. However, I couldn't allow people who meant nothing in my life to hinder my goals. I joined the YMCA and Curves. Each had a different purpose. Through personal and specialized training and meals, I discovered my own way. I ended up becoming a pescetarian, then vegetarian, and by 2013 I had become a full vegan. I was losing weight, looking good, and feeling great. I went from walking to finally running a full 1.5 miles nonstop. The accomplishments were little, but great in my mind. I knew that a healthy lifestyle was just as much about mindset as anything, and I was grateful for the process of taking my mind back to enhance my mental and physical health.

Spirituality

I spent five years engulfing myself in ministry. I attended singles conferences, Girls Night Out Events, singles workshops, Bible study, etc. I returned to the foundation that my parents raised me in...church. I really didn't want to be in the church, but once I stepped in the door it felt natural. On January 5, 2012, I attended a singles workshop called "How to Handle Yourself in the Process." Listen...this is what the church needs to be teaching. But instead, we skip the most important topics in youth service like love, sex, betrayal, manipulation, good versus bad attention, etc. They talk about the lust of the eye, the lust of the flesh, but can we really get into what that means and what temptation looks like out here in the real world? Like let's talk about porn and masturbation. I know that's too much for the "church folk", but it's real. I had to shed myself of all these things during my five-year journey of self-healing. I didn't want any distractions, toxic relationships or bad habits.

12

I Thought He Was the One

"God, I thank you for Nigel Ambique. I ask that you wrap your arms around him from this day forward and direct his path. You have anointed him with many talents and served him grace and mercy at a time in his life when he needed You the most. God, he knows You, but I ask that You let him know that you are his father and that you love him more than he will ever know. When times get confusing, give him clarity, when his heart is hardened, soften it with your love, when he seeks the love and presence of his biological father, let him know that you are there. Remove all fear from his heart so that the greatness you have placed in him will come out. Place good men in his path that are of You to help guide him and give him good Godly friendships. For when he feels like he is wavering they can gird him up. Take away the pain I have in the flesh from my broken heart, and take over in the spirit so I can help him through You. Increase his capacity to love and show love to him just as You have shown to us. In Jesus Name, Amen."

For those who knew our love story, it was hard to see how it ended. We were the epitome of black love. Where you saw him, you saw me and vice versa. The end was a trauma that I never saw based off the beginning. I was there in every way possible. I cooked. I cleaned. I gave to this man every part of me there was to give physically, emotionally, mentally, spiritually and financially, but in the end that was not enough. It was not enough for him to commit. To know that I was the one.

We met on a college campus in Pennsylvania. I was working as a full-time administrator, and he had just started graduate school and lived on the main campus. Our department was interviewing for a student position, and our boss told us we were interviewing a graduate student. He walked in, dressed well, nice smile, well spoken, and very confident. He was definitely over 6'0, chocolate complexion, wide shoulders, stocky, and he had a unique accent. I wasn't even looking at him that way at first. How could I when my coworker's big head was in the way during interviews as we sat around an oval shaped conference table? I could hear his voice, he could hear mine, but we didn't see each other at all outside of his initial entrance into the room. The next day, I was walking out of the Student Union Building from my office and a tall, dark, handsome man was walking in. Professionally dressed with a Louis Vuitton briefcase. We passed each other in the crowd of students, but we must have felt something because we both paused as soon as we cleared each other and looked back for a split second. It was weird, definitely like something from a movie. I didn't even realize it was him because I didn't get a good look at his face in the interview, only his silhouette.

The next day when I came to the office, my coworker was training him and officially introduced me to him. He shook my hand, locked eyes with me, and cracked a sexy smirk as he said "Nice to meet you." I was coming in the room to ask my coworker if he could help me set up for a training I had to do for the department that night. My coworker said he wasn't free and I had already asked everyone else. I couldn't move those tables alone. Nigel told me he would help me. He told me he would call me when he got to the building to help me set up. He started looking on the desk for a piece of paper. He tore it in two and wrote his number down and handed it to me. In my head I was thinking, I hope this grown man has a cell phone…it's 2013. I didn't want to be rude so I wrote my phone number on the other piece of paper, thanked him and told him I would see him later.

We were supposed to have an indoor date night, but the time kept getting later. It started to turn me off. I texted him and asked him what time he was coming and he said around 9 p.m. That time came and went. About 45 minutes later he called me and said he was at my door. I was very uptight and didn't expect him to stay long. When he entered my apartment, he immediately complimented my décor. He said it was very nice and felt like home. We made our way to the living room. He sat on the couch and I sat on the sofa. My hospitality went out the window that night because my mind was set on get in, get out. He was smiling, light hearted and ready to enjoy the evening and I was uptight. He smiled at me and asked, "Can I have something to drink?" In my head I thought no, but I'm a nice girl, so I went to the kitchen, opened the refrigerator and said "sure." My apartment was an open concept, so he watched me bend down into the refrigerator and as I came back up, I noticed his warm body behind me. He was still smiling and seemed very comfortable. Then he looked in my refrigerator as the door was opened and said "Oh I see you have pink miscato...let's have some of that." I poured him a glass and he asked where was mine. I poured a little and he took the bottle and poured an adult portion into my cup.

We sat, drank, and talked all night. We didn't get to any games or movies. We talked about everything from church, family, Greek life, hobbies, college, future goals, and Lincoln. By the time we came up for breath it was almost 5am. We were so engulfed in the conversation we never even mentioned food or the bathroom.

We both stood up. Nigel smiled and said, "You know we have been here this whole time and you haven't given me a tour." Honestly, my apartment wasn't that big, so I wasn't sure what he wanted to tour. He seemed cool, so I obliged. We started with the kitchen and I gave him a tour. When we reached the bedroom, I pointed to the door and said "And that's my bedroom." He was like "You aren't going to show me your bedroom? You have such nice décor in the rest of your place; I know you bedroom must look nice too. I don't have to see the whole thing, just let me peek." I held the door ajar and flipped the light switch on the wall. I don't know what it was about my room, but as soon as he looked at my bed he got excited. As we stood in the doorway with his warm body behind mine looking over my shoulder, he came closer and held me tight. It was so soothing and felt just right. I quickly snapped out of it because it felt too right. I was not trying to go down this road again, so I was thinking of ways to keep it happy and light. He started kissing on me and walked back to the living room still holding on tight to my hips. When we got to the couch he started grinding on me, kissing my neck and breathing hard in my ear. I told him I wasn't ready for all of that and he respectfully surrendered.

Time passed, and I was making an impact on his life physically, emotionally, and spiritually. It was indescribable and envied by many. When we first met, I was a vegetarian, and he tried a vegetarian lifestyle with me. We lost so much weight. We were looking good and feeling good. We were inseparable. The Thanksgiving that we dated, which was 2013, he went home for break to be with his family. That was normal for a holiday, but he couldn't stand to be away from me. We talked on the phone the entire the time. He grew to love me more when I won the heart of his mother. He had just gotten a refund check around that time and wanted to make his money last, but he also wanted to spoil his mom. So I sent him a financial breakdown within 5 minutes of him venting to me which including an item line to buy groceries for his mom and spoil her with some holiday shopping. She told him I was a good catch.

Break was over and we both returned to campus to welcome the students back. I couldn't wait to see him and he was even more excited to see me.

"I missed you so much" he said.

"I missed you too."

He was a gentleman from the start. He took my coat off (he always put my coat on and zipped/buttoned it as well as took it off). After hanging my coat up he took his off too.

"How much did you miss me?"

"How much did you miss me?" he smiled.

He held my hand in his, gazed into my eyes and stayed there until we saw the twinkle in each other's pupils.

"Being away from you for a week felt like longer. Maybe next time I can come with you."

He let go of my hand and made his way to the couch. We were about to eat, so he made himself comfortable. I didn't know what to think. He was great, but I was still in my healing process. Everything was going smooth when I wasn't faced with temptation, but now I was back in the field. The food was already cooked. I plated it and walked over to join Nigel so we could eat. We continued small talk throughout dinner, which led to watching a movie, then me dosing off in his arms.

He kissed me and said "Tiph. It's getting late."

I sat up on the couch trying to force my eyelids to open. I didn't mean to fall asleep. It was 4am.

"I don't want to leave. Can I stay here?"

I didn't even think before I replied, "Yes."

Our bond grew fast. The more time we spent together, the less he wanted to be apart. It was never boring. And things were starting to heat up.

When we woke up the next day, Nigel laid in bed with me just talking like we always do. He was an intellect, so our conversations were always thought provoking and entertaining.

Nigel was a freak. I could tell by the way he kissed, but normally he was able to restrain himself. He climbed on top of me, grabbed my butt, and lifted me around his waist. I was in disbelief. This was really happening to me again. All I could think was "dang neither one of us have a condom." I wanted to tell him to wait. I wanted to stop altogether. I had come such a long way. It's hard to fight the flesh. He was hitting every spot just right. As he entered deeper into my abyss, his body came closer to mine. I could feel all of him giving his all to me. It was the first time I felt like a man was actually making love to me. He was gentle, he was sensual, and he was romantic in every move and moan that he made. He rolled to the right of me, placed my right thigh over his leg and entered me in a different position. Once again I was in bliss. Everything went out the window as I let out a soft moan in response to his pleasure.

As Nigel got close to his climax, his stroke sped up and his grip got firmer. I don't know where my trigger came from, but my eyes opened, my assertiveness peaked, and tears started to roll down my face. He was confused. He thought it was him.

"Are you okay?" he asked softly. "Tell me what's wrong. Is it something I did?"

I didn't know how to answer him. So many thoughts and emotions ran through my head. I had never told anyone what happened to me. Not even my mom, and everyone knows how close we are. Tears continued to roll down my face in silence. He laid there staring at me in confusion yet sincerity. I couldn't get the words to come out.

"Tiph…" he said. "Talk to me."

I took a deep gulp. A pause. Another gulp. And then I felt as ready as I was going to be. I wanted him to know all of me and me all of him. He was different and I was older, so I had to start this off the right way. I told Nigel about my relationship from chapter 7 and how it ended in rape. He didn't know what to do or say. He just held me in his arms, told me he was sorry I went through that, and that everything would be ok.

He had naturally muscular arms. His grip was firm yet gentle. I let out a sigh of relief. I was still getting to know him, but something felt right...something felt different. It became one of my favorite places in the world. His arms made me feel secure.

We became best friends. Literally, we did everything together. He didn't drive though, so I was the driver for all of our spontaneous outings and dates.

The spring of 2014 I began looking for other jobs. I knew it would change our relationship because we were use to being in such close proximity to each other, but he gave me his support to pursue better opportunities. After being the final candidate for several colleges in the VA, PA and DE areas, I decided to take a job outside of the Pittsburgh area.

That summer was rough. He went back to work at a

camp in upstate New York, while I held things down in PA. I had just started my doctoral program, and he was still pursuing his Masters. With no Internet access where he was working, I took on his workload and mine. I didn't think it would be that bad because his class was solely online. However, with work and two rigorous course loads, I decided to withdrawal from my class, defer my admission to the fall and focus on his course since he was in the middle of his cohort.

I started my new job in August 2014. During that time, he also accepted a full-time position at the college we currently served. I was on the west side of Pennsylvania and he was on the east. We managed to make it work, but I had no idea that this would be the start of the decline of us.

December 2014, he brought me a heart-shaped rose gold and diamond ring for Christmas. He was so excited about picking this ring out with my mom and he promised me that he would be upgrading it to the real thing real soon. Our lives were blissful, the sex was great, and our friendship was unmatched. We rang in 2015 together in church and knew that with him graduating with his masters this year, we would be taking our relationship to the next level.

On January 31, 2015, a turn of events in my family

through our relationship for a loop. He was the one who took the call from my mom. He was there for me through it all. The only thing is, things started getting worse. The experience hit some triggers of hurt for him and me that we both thought we grew through. It was a lot to take in. We were changing, growing, and fighting the turmoil of life that tried to plague our relationship. We hung in there. We even started reading a book together called *Making Good Habits, Breaking Bad Habits* by Joyce Meyer. My church was reading it corporately. He loved my church. He was always open to trying new things with me, so we read the book together. It was a lot going on. I had resigned from my job in Pittsburgh and was unemployed, we were having family issues, I was still recovering from a major surgery, and he was nearing graduation.

In March 2015, we attended the wedding of one of his closest friends in Allentown, Pennsylvania. We got into an argument. He aggressively uttered, "If you walk out the door you're done!" I walked out with all of my things and closed the door as a tear rolled down my left cheek. I waited downstairs in the lobby staring out of the window at the treacherous rainstorm outside. I sat in the lobby of the Hyatt Hotel, watching guest walk by smiling while I was crumbling inside. After two hours, I texted his phone and told him that I wanted to come upstairs to talk. We argued loud and hard. Then he locked himself in the bathroom of the room we stayed in, letting out his rage of every emotion every way he knew how. When the door opened, he stood there crying. He hit the floor, crawled over to me sitting on the couch, and laid his head in my lap. Through his tears he cried out

"I don't want to lose you…I can't do this without you."

We were growing more distant than ever. I knew it was bad when graduation continued to near and I didn't hear much from him about his announcement or tickets. He had never been to a concert, so I wanted to do something special for him. They were having an old school concern in Atlantic City the weekend of his graduation. I figured with his family coming to town we could spend a couple days with them, then head out Saturday night for the concert and stay overnight in AC. I borrowed the money from my mom since I wasn't working and planned the trip. The closer we got to graduation, the more I started to ask him about tickets and logistics. I ended up breaking the surprise to him because he was being so secretive. When I told him, he wasn't exactly thrilled. He said that I shouldn't plan surprises without consulting the person first. I didn't understand that because that defeats the point of a surprise. We ended up in an argument. It was then that I found out that I also didn't have a ticket to his graduation. I asked about the overflow area and he said he would see what he could do.

I knew this feeling oh too well. I tried to ignore the hurt. I pressed through hard because I loved this man. I worked hard on myself and even harder on us. He was different than the others. I just knew he was my forever. I did everything I could to be there for him. I took him to parks and serene settings to see if that would help him let loose. I was trying to avoid what I knew. He was ending a major chapter of his life and walking in fear into the next. He had shut down on me.

Since a few members from his family couldn't come to graduation, I ended up with a ticket. We weren't on the best terms, but I was so proud of him, and nothing could change what we had been through. Since his family left the same day, he ended up going to the concert with me so I didn't lose the money I had already put out. We had a good time, but the vibe was very different for us both.

When we returned home he was distant. I gave him space. In my hurt I let him go, praying that it would only help us stay together. I was still there when he was ready.

Days turned to weeks and communication was to a minimum. Being the initiator I am, I asked to take him on a date so we could talk. We went to a local park. He raced me to the swings. I thought that I did it. That I tapped into his emotions. He opened up to me about the men in his family and his father. It was hard, but I was there for him just as he was there for me. The atmosphere shifted though. It was different. No matter how much love, time, gifts, sex, support, etc. I gave him, it wasn't enough. He wasn't ready for me to be there for him. He didn't know how to grow past what he was feeling...how to shake this stage of his life. He was emotionally unavailable to me. I couldn't understand it. I should've though because that was me. Loved but empty. It started with me and though I had grown over the course of my five-year healing journey, I had met my match...in more ways than one. I knew only God could help him through and the support of other men could help him through this. So I gave him a break to be alone. I told him I would still be here. But that led to weeks and months. As I prayed for him, God laid on my heart the number 8. His birthday was September 8th. So I called him and told him that he could take as much time as he need until his birthday. If I hear from him I know our love will carry us through. If I don't that will be the start of a new beginning for us both. Needless to say he became a chapter in this book so we didn't work out. That was the first time I actually felt my heart.

13

Closure

C losure doesn't always come the way we want. Sometimes it doesn't come at all. Other times it comes, but we become in denial because we were blindsided.

As I looked back at my life, I had finally accepted it. All of it. I was the one who said I'd never be her, but here I am. They say "karma is a b****." That little church girl who judged those around me who got pregnant at the age of 14. I judged the teen girls because their moms were judging me. No kids, but this life of chasing acceptance through giving the one thing I thought would keep a man had overtaken me. Closure starts with your mindset. Below are some of the steps I took to gain closure.

#1 – Cut off contact

In chapter 12, the first thing I did after realizing Nigel wasn't ready was create distance.

#2 – Get rid of everything from old relationships

That box you have in your closet with those fortune cookies from old dates, folded notes, teddy bears, even that ring…get rid of it! Trust me, I know how you feel. I have been there.

#3 – Set boundaries with your ex if you have to be around each other

Full disclosure: Nigel and I became coworkers a few years after we broke up. It wasn't easy at first, but we both set healthy boundaries and were able to have a great working relationship.

#4 – Write a goodbye letter

This was so therapeutic for me. I found an old Valentine's and wrote the letter on that. It wasn't even filled out by the man who purchased it for me. It made me reflect on a few things. I penned the things I learned about him and myself in the card then mailed it to him. That closed that chapter of my book.

#5 – Forgiveness

Forgiveness is a process, but in order to gain total freedom, your must work to forgive your ex. Before you can get to this step, you must first forgive yourself. Work through your emotions, frustrations, questions and fears. This task is easier said than done.

#6 – Seek God

This step goes without explanation. When my alignment with God is off, my decision-making is altered. Seeking God allowed you to gain a sense of peace that will surpass any understand that we will try to make out of the situation. Our minds are programmed to replay memories of hurt and pain, but God can heal your heart better than any man or woman.

#7 – Get to Work

Often times when we are in relationships, we lose ourselves in the process of being in love. The journey of falling in love is blinding, but it is important to get back to you after a break up. Find a hobby, start a business, go for that promotion. This takes time, but it is important in getting back on track. Seek God first and allow him to direct your next move, then get to work!

14

Intentional Healing

I shut down hard. Deep down I knew I had to keep moving. I turned to the only source I knew. It was frustrating. As I was reading Proverbs 3:5-6 in my Women's Devotional Bible, I began to cry. I continued reading, trying to ignore the voice within repeatedly saying, you have to love him...you have to continue to love him with the same love that I love you. I paused in confusion, and slight anger because my heart was broken. But I took a deep breath and thanked God for his love, comfort, and healing. The healing process from the breakup with Nigel was tough. It was through this process that I realized my relationships in the past didn't work out because of me physically, but because of the lack of Christ's love within the men I was intimate with. The hurt was unbearable. The day that we broke up, I asked him why he changed so much, and he told me that I was ready for a relationship, but he wasn't. Each day that passed, I kept reading his last message to me, and I realized that he was not the first guy to tell me that. He told me that I was the first person in his life that loved him and showed him through action outside of the women in his family. At the time he was thirty-one years old. He said that he knew he wants to get married one day, he just didn't know if I was the one he was supposed to marry. Instead of blaming myself this time, I took ownership. I thought about the prayer warriors in my life that prayed for me since I was in my mother's womb. I thought about the sleepless nights and early mornings my mom sacrificed praying for me, but more importantly, I reflected on the actions of love and culture that my mom created for our household and how I recreated that in the relationships I was in.

It is easy to shut down when you are hurt. To think you are not good enough, to find fault, and vow to never do the things again that caused you heartbreak. Well this time that was over. Once I realized that I was the one who had shown so many people love and grew to understand unconditional love, not through my thighs, but accepting them as they were in life, I realized that it was not a time to run, it was a time to fight for the next level of love. I began to pray to God to restore me, forgive me and heal me to allow me to show the His love to those I come in contact with.

At the end of it all, I cleared a space in my bedroom and made it my temple, my war room, and my motivation. I placed declarations, goals and scriptures on my double closet doors and recited them each time I looked over. But Proverbs 31 was one that I longed to embody. As I read it, I laid both of my hands on the chapter and asked God to make her me. I realized that He gave me the blueprint; I just had to seek Him to execute it. I'm not perfect. As you can tell from this book, and I still have a lot of growth, but once I really understood that I am fearfully and wonderfully made, doors began to shut and open for me. This was the start of my healing.

Healing

I was so tired of meeting people in my personal life

that it showed in my attitude. My family did their best to help me cope, but God knew better than anyone my next steps. When I met him I was shy, but he wasn't. There was a certain heir he brought to any room he entered. His smile, the way he moved, his very presence could transform the ambience of any environment. He would make his way around the room greeting everyone with smiles and hugs.

As the crowd dissipated he made his way to the room I was in. Sitting alone on the couch. The aura changed as soon as our vibes connected. My darkness dampened him, but he sat down anyway and stared. I finally looked up and caught his eye. He cracked a smile, but I did not budge, so he sat there in my silence to himself. It was a four-year-old little boy. My (now) nephew was a major part in my healing.

One day he was sitting at the kitchen island in my mother's house playing a game on his iPad. I had just walked in from a long day of running my business, and he wanted my help with this game so bad. As I bent down closer to his face to help him, I felt his eyes move away from the screen, looking at the side of my face. A look that I learned was him looking deeper into my heart. I knew if I looked at him I would cry, so I focused in hard at the iPad screen. After the longest sixty seconds of my life, he said

"Tiphane` are you ok?" and gave me a soft kiss on my left cheek. Doing my best to hold back tears, I had to excuse myself to the bathroom located right off the kitchen to release the pain I kept bottled up inside. The truth is that I was not okay, but how could I express that or why to my four-year-old nephew? A four year old saw right through me, but also lifted me up in more ways than he knows. It was on this day that I understood why so many girls have kids seeking unconditional love. But I knew that it was really the love of God shown through the innocence of a child that warmed my heart.

Health

Exercise has been proven to relieve stress and depression. There are so many endorphins released when working out. That is one thing that helped me on my journey to heal from such massive heartache. I was committed to walking outside everyday. During my walks I would pray, listen to music and be presently present in the scenery of nature along the trail. My mom watched me as I grew through my pain. One day she decided to leave out right after me. I guess it was mother's intuition. I was still walking, but she decided to pick her pace to a jog, so she passed me. As I zoned out to my surrounding scenery, a worship song rang through the headphone of the playlist on my iPod. I felt like something had knocked the wind out of me. I burst into tears on the side of the road and slowly dropped to my knees. My mom turned around slowly. As she saw me down on the ground she jogged to my aid. I couldn't control my breathing and the tears would not stop flowing. She stopped and prayed with me. My health was helping me heal. I had to take care of my body as well as my mind. The thing I was putting in was helping cleanse me just as much as the movements I was doing. I was losing weight from the inside out.

Spirituality

"Lord, thank You for using me as a vessel to be an angel of love for Your children who needed it the most. Thank You for making me unique, and filling me with enough unconditional love to shown through action love to others the way You have show it to me. Thank You for giving me the strength to endure the hurt I have experienced and love others and myself through the process of it all. Now that my eyes have been opened, send me someone to love, but first prepare me to have the capacity to receive it. I ask that You touch the hearts of all the men I have loved and replace the love between my thighs with the love of Christ. Open their eyes, remove their fear, humble them before You, and give them the capacity to receive You here on this earth through the next beacon of light You send in their path to love them. Amen."

He gave me the words to pray over the men who have hurt me and the strongholds and soul ties that have come into my life. After the prayer these words resonated within me, "Your life is about to crescendo into a symphony of praise. When His plan crescendos, you will be glad you didn't settle for your own way. He is up to something. Do not miss it!"

Self-Actualization

I took a look deep within. I remember God revealing the number 8 to me, so I prayed that he show me 8 areas where I lacked in my relationship with Nigel. I wanted to learn from this relationship as much as I could. I fasted and prayed for 8 days. Each day I read Proverbs 31. I placed my hands on the pages and ask God to make me more like her. Each day a lesson hit my spirit about my relationship. And the last day was the prayer I wrote for him that I placed at the beginning of this chapter. God revealed his hurt to me while I was dealing with my own.

Lessons Learned

Lesson 1: The problem with us is that we are taught when you find someone to share your life with, you build memories with that person. While that is true, it is also true that you are still two individual people. So, there will be some memories that you will build by yourself, even when you are married, and that is okay. I am one that wants to share and give to everyone all the great things I have experienced...vacation spots, great restaurants, movies, outdoor activities, etc. It would be wrong to say that you can't find a person who is down with all of that, but it would also be false hope for me to say that you are going to find a person that wants to go to all those places with you ALL the time. Stop feeling left out. You came in this world alone, and you will leave this world alone despite the greatest friend you have or your true love/soul mate. And that my friend is why God says not to be unequally yoked. You see, as children of God, we were taught the spiritual side of being unequally yoked, but what about the rest? In order to be mature enough to have experience and build memories outside of your companionship, you have to set boundaries.

Lesson 2: When things get old, we tend to look for something new. It's not our fault; this is the society we live in. When the latest phone comes out, everyone wants to buy it. And if you don't have the latest and greatest people look at you funny. My customers talk about me all the time for still carrying an iPhone 4. But what they don't know is that carrying this phone did more for me than just reppin the brand of my own business. It taught me that sometimes in life we are in such a hurry to get to the next best thing that we look past the same product of something just because it is an older model. Let's go back to the basics. "If it ain't broke, don't fix it." Now that does not mean don't develop it and grow with it. Even older models of the iPhones have software updates. It's because Apple realized that no matter how old a version of their product is, it still needs improvement. This same concept goes for us as humans. Yes your age brings you wisdom through life's experience, but no matter the age of a person, we all need continuous improvement. Most small-minded people would look at this concept as change, and once they hit a certain age claim that nobody can "change" them. However, many people with vision, wealth and wisdom would understand that this needed concept is called personal development. The reality is, the world around us changes and evolves daily, so why would you not want to do like businesses are forced to do and keep up with that same current. You do not have to conform to the world and in the ever so changing societal norms; develop spiritually if that's your thing; develop intellectually, or financially, but the most important thing is to develop. Why you ask? Because without vision people perish. But you can't form and keep a clear vision if you are idle.

15

Young Love

I wish you knew the scar you left on my heart. You were supposed to teach me how to love and receive love. I'd be lying if I said I forgave you, but I'm working on it.

He was the young love I should've experienced when I was younger. We were five years apart, but willing to give each other a shot. I was nearing thirty and ready to settle down, whereas he was just getting started with his twenties and ready to explore what life had to offer. We met in Germantown at a business event. I was the guest speaker for the evening. I remember asking the crowd who they thought my first client was when I started my own business; Kalvin spoke out of the crowd "Your boyfriend." I paused for a moment knowing that I didn't have a man in my life. "Uh no. Good guess though." Before he left, we scheduled to meet up at his house the next day to go over some business logistics.

I was assigned as his mentor, but something seemed deeper than that from the start. He was "that dude." The guy that you described to your best friend during late night conversations. The one that doesn't compliment you at all, but adds value to every area of your life plus the ones you never even thought about. But, to understand our relationship, I needed to understand wants versus needs. A concept that Kalvin embedded deep within me, but I realized I truly didn't understand what that meant for my life, so I became his teacher in business and he became my teacher in life.

My first encounter with Kalvin was all business. I wasn't even looking at him to get to know him on a personal level, but he had peeped me out from the start. Teaching him about posture when speaking to others only drew him closer to me as a woman. He grew a strong connection for me, but he knew that he would only hurt me if he got too close.

Over time, I learned his true intentions and I grew to

love Kalvin deeper than any man I had ever met in my twenty-eight years of life. Not because he loved me enough to let me go, but because he loved me enough to cherish me and value my worth enough to know that I deserved to be with a man better than he could be for me at that time. Our relationship was a roller coaster of confusion, and that's exactly how this chapter is about to flow. There is no simple way to put it. No clear path to us. No steady timeline of events. We were all over the place. Mainly because I was still hurting...more than I knew. So sit back, buckle up and brace yourself for the chapter 14 ride of *The Love Between My Thighs*.

Our first meet up on a personal level was a bust. I should've left him then. It was a gloomy, rainy Wednesday morning. We were supposed to meet up at his house. Just the short walk from my garage to my car at the end of the driveway left me drenched. I started my car, turned on my windshield wipers and realized that this was worse than I thought. I could barely see sitting idle, yet alone drive down 95. I must've been desperate for companionship because I went anyway. The drive sucked! I was squinting the entire time, and was beyond irritated. I had an hour and fifteen minute drive.

When I pulled up I called Kalvin's phone. It was going

straight to voicemail. I was cool at first, but after about thirty minutes I started blowing him up through text and calls. He finally contacted me back and told me that he wasn't home. He said he forgot. I sat back in my driver's seat in disbelief. I didn't know anyone in that part of Philly that was home at that time of day. Everyone was working. Now I was definitely pissed. I texted Kalvin and told him my situation, but all he could say was sorry.

I pulled my phone out and looked up the closest Panera Bread on Google. I wasn't about to go all the way back to Delaware in this rain, plus I had other business to handle in Philly that evening. Panera Bread was twenty-five minutes away, so I braced my eyes for the drive and kept it moving. As soon as I pulled up to Panera Bread, one of my business partners in Philly called and asked if I could go over some things with her. I wasn't doing anything anyway, and I needed to get my mind off of everything so we agreed to meet on City Line Avenue. I took that ride, another thirty-five minutes from where I was, only for her to stand me up. I sat in my car crying. I was over it. I gathered myself, walked in the Chili's restaurant and treated myself to dinner for one before my next meeting. It felt like the longest dinner ever as I gazed out the blurry window into the gloomy parking lot.

After dinner, I made my way to my next meeting. When I parked, I felt down. I knew I couldn't even fake a smile at this point in the day. I sat there for a while trying to get myself together. I needed someone to enhance my mood. I don't know what made me do this, but I called my last comfort zone...Nigel. He actually picked up. I just sat there breathing in his ear.

"Tiph..." he said gently.

Tears began to roll down my left cheek. He could tell I was crying, but I was completely silent.

"Tiph...Are you..."

I hung up on him before he could say anything. I couldn't stand to talk to him either. He hurt me. I felt alone. I was pissed off, sad and tired at this point, but I had to keep moving...business called.

Kalvin and I went back to strictly business. I had to keep moving. I couldn't let him affect my money. He knew he messed up and he tried to redeem himself. I had some business meetings with a few males in Philly and he volunteered to meet me there and help out so I didn't have to go alone. Afterwards, he treated me to Jamaican food for lunch because he knew I was scheduled to have a long day.

Time flew and the grind continued, but I was still on Kalvin's mind. He asked to meet up for Christmas. We went to Willow Grove Mall. I looked nice, but he could've definitely done better. It's disheartening to look at a tall, dark man with no dress game, but that was Kalvin. As we walked around the mall he kept asking me what I wanted for Christmas, but my mind wasn't on that, however, he was determined. He said I had to pick something from any store or we weren't leaving until I he bought me something. I wasn't impressed with money or gifts even though that's how I expressed my love, so I picked something simple so we could move on.

Our bond built from there. We rang in 2016 with a call to each other yelling "Turnip!" Not party style, but with our goals and business ventures.

We were doing well, but Kalvin noticed more about me than I thought. Early on in our relationship he told me he wanted to make me a soldier. He said, "I don't know how to say this but...you're soft. You're soft, but you're hard. I mean you're hard...but you're soft". I was offended and a little confused. I thought I was invincible, or at least that's what everyone around me led me to believe. I knew I was a powerhouse...businesswoman, career driven, creative, the whole nine. I had the courage to run into any situation big or small, dark or light and come out on top. But even in my mental and physical strength, I lacked emotional strength, and Kalvin was determined to change that. "Nobody can touch you anymore physically or emotionally," he said as he reached to put my hand in his.

I wanted him to be my companion, but he needed me to be his friend and he be mine to protect me. All he wanted to do was teach me the game of chess, but I wasn't as up to speed on the game of life.

The more street smarts he taught me, the more I became engaged with him. Every time he felt me getting close to him, he tried to run by breaking up with me, but I chased him. I thought that I could love him into being comfortable around me.

Kalvin knew he was no good to me as a boyfriend. He knew that the closer we got romantically, he would only hurt me in the long run. He called me and told me he didn't want a relationship. He just wanted to be friends. Although Kalvin made the decision to just be friends, and the conversation was filled with tears and a lot of emotion, I knew that it was growth and unconditional love. For once I had a man that was trying to shield me from hurt, but I ran head first into it.

He stayed around after the breakup. We were tied financially. Being around each other made us an on again off again relationship. But over time, I got back to being me. Fitness became a priority again, and he wanted to get his personal trainer certification, so it worked out great. While visiting my mom one nice spring day, I decided to do some Yoga and strength training on her deck out back. She came outside to join me, but her motive was to talk to me about Kalvin.

Without hesitation she just came out and said,

"Tiphane what do you see in him. He is ugly and he's not on your level. It's something about him. I can't really tell you everything, but I know he's not right for you."

"But I dated someone on my level" I responded. Nigel. He looked great on paper. He was pursuing his second degree. He was physically appeasing, friendly, family oriented...the whole nine. He was mature in age, but he wasn't ready."

I was hurt by the conversation with my mom. I was confused at this point. I felt like no matter what I looked for in a man I was wrong. I eventually told Kalvin about the conversation, and he agreed. He said I should listen to my mom, but I saw the potential in him...that's where I went wrong.

I finally wore him down and he opened up to me.

"I got in a relationship because I knew what I wanted and I'm the kind of guy that locks in and once I'm locked in I'm loaded. I wanted someone I could build with grow with. I made a decision that I'm very proud of. I just want to grow, look grow, learn grow, argue grow, be silent grow, but I'm not the guy for you."

We got back together. This time we were going strong. We both got into positions in our careers, he got a new car, business was moving, we were complimenting each other and living freely. By this time, our birthdays were approaching. His was in September and mine in October. I wanted to go Niagara Falls, but all of my friends backed out. Kalvin promised to take me. I was hesitant because I was use to being let down. He said "Trust me…I got you goes a long way." I smiled and anxiously got back into planning my big day.

Needless to say, I gave him everything he never had for his birthday, and he gave me tears and heartache on mine. I always opened up my heart to this, and it was no different this time. The one thing I told him that I did not want for my birthday is what I got. I sat in my apartment alone. No Niagara Falls, not even a 2 for $20 dinner, or a cooked meal at home.

As I sat there and cried, I wrote in my journal.
October 2, 2016 "Is it me? Do I seek too much? Or not enough? Is it that I am not vocal enough? I don't

understand why it's so hard for others to give me what I give them. When the negative energy of the world around me drains my productivity, wake me up and rejuvenate my vision of the world around us. Breakfast in bed. Even if it were a waffle, heck a piece of toast or a bagel with strawberry cream cheese would be nice. To pop in a movie at the house and make a meal out of the food in the cabinets. I don't need the world, but I do need more. I'm stuck between feeling ungrateful and settling. And every time that happens on the inside I'm melting. I don't know if I'm not good enough, or if these things are just fantasies not meant for me. You've sung to people and posted on FB, but I get no shout out on my birthday. Maybe I'm the encourager of dreams but not the person to share the end!"

The negligence of his actions from my birthday led to major arguments. It wasn't what broke us up. We were already a game of cat and mouse, but this was the final ending to it all. Even in my anger and his guilt, we built a bond that I'll never forget. He broke up with me one last time, but in my anger I revealed something to him that caught his eye. He always thought I was radiantly beautiful, but through my pain, he could hear that's not how I felt inside.

He took me by the hand and led me to my bathroom

mirror and told me to look deep inside. I refused the woman in front of me for many reasons. He held my arms to my side and said softly,

"You taught me posture, now it's my turn to teach you the true value that you possess inside."

Turning my head from side to side, I tried to avoid the reflection before me. I literally just stood there and cried. Eventually I caught a glimpse of her. All I could do is stare at every tear that fell from my eyes. The puddles forming on the bathroom sink were building up from the pain I held back for so long inside of me.

He started undressing me, which was weird timing to me. He walked me to my bathroom door where my full body mirror hung over the door. There I stood. Naked...in every sense of it's meaning. Faced with every curve, crevice, and flaw of my mocha chocolate body. Every cellulite, bump, curve, blemish, flab, roll was there. I was naked in a body length mirror...the most venerable I had ever been. I avoided mirrors for so long, but Kalvin forced me to see my beauty from within.

As much as we went through I tried to hold out, but I fell once again. I opened my thighs to let him love my inner abyss, but this time, I didn't just leave with scars, I stayed with growth within myself, learning, and love still on the table. Even though my actions were not pleasing in the eyes of God, I didn't regret this one like I did the others. I was convicted, but not restricted by my decision because I learned and grew in more ways than I did before.

The breakup was hard, but losing a friend was even harder. While I was forcing the relationship I wanted, I was destroying the relationship I needed. A true friendship. I wanted a relationship, but was not focused on finding one. He wanted a friend, but was not focused on finding one. We both met each other at dark times in our lives, but we were pushing to greatness, not realizing that we needed the lessons, wisdom, compassion, companionship, prayers and reliability of each other.

16

Life Rant

D o you want to know how I REALLY felt about opening up my heart and thighs to a man after going through such heartache? Before reflecting and seeking God I went through a period of doubt, grief, confusion, frustration and a mix of other emotions. I felt like an idiot or that I was dumb for even continuing to talk to him. At the beginning everything I learned in my healing process from my previous relationship had kicked in and I was cool, calm and collective. All I wanted to do was love and support him. Each time he called and I saw his name I would roll my eyes and try to figure out where I went wrong and why I kept attracting the same type of men in my life. I mean how many times can you trust someone who tells you they're different after talks about the future? I didn't want to see him because I felt like I was chasing him. I overthought everything he said from that day on. I backed up because I doubted that he wanted me. The first time he requested to video chat me I declined out of anger.

***

That night Kalvin texted me at 1:32am "Still up"? Although I wanted to talk to him, I realized that I had to have boundaries in this newfound "friendship" that he asked for, so I decided not to converse with him that night even though I was awake. When I woke up in the morning, I had a message in my inbox from Kalvin that read:

"Jus up thinkn bout u and I wanna say, I gotchu goooooooes a looooong way! And I love u everyday for being u, and when u read ya book to me I teared up and all I could do was smile! Im happy/proud! And when u said u didn't cry I knew like yea she really dot! Gn even tho I make shit hard, I promise you all smiles and happiness! The pain is NOT in vain, if I spelled that right, gn your highness! #bosslady"

I knew that I was promised a life of smiles and happiness because God said so in Jeremiah 29:11. I knew that I could find comfort in God, but what hurt the most was the uncertainty of who my Boaz would be to give me smiles and happiness on earth. Kalvin promised me smiles and happiness, but not from him. Was he going to sit back and allow another man to come into my life and be ok with that? Was he going to fight for me like he said he would?

Wants vs. Needs

Have you ever looked at yourself through someone else's eyes? I know what you're thinking...impossible right? Wrong. We live in a society filled with messengers that pass us daily. Some may come in the form of a smile, a hello, a simple conversation, others may come in a more in depth way. No matter how it comes, these are all forms of seeing yourself through the eyes of everyone else in the world. They are letting you know if you are welcoming, happy, on the right track, etc. I remember the day I saw myself in the mirror for the first time. The truest reflection I have ever seen in my life.

Becoming a mental warrior is a journey. It was on this day that the mirror not only showed me but spoke to me.

"Maybe I'm built for something different. I'm just not sure what. I look at pictures of my friend's and their families and I want that bond, but at the same time, I don't. Often times I don't know who I am or why I'm here, but I know that if I just keep moving, one day I will run into it or it will run into me. Most days I don't love myself because I struggle understanding myself. I took so much time off to learn about me. To give myself away spiritually. Only to open up and be broken after giving so much of my overcompensating love language again. All I know is that I do great things and people think I'm awesome. Some days I think I am too, until I end up with the short end of the stick. Why can't I breathe, feel, smell the romance, or come close to being shown the treatment everyone says I deserve?"

For today, I'll just try to dig deep for happiness and know that the desires of my heart have not yet found me. I won't be sung to, held, given a collage of pictures, kissed endlessly, made breakfast, etc. It's just another day. Another day for me to keep it moving and just be grateful to God that he has kept me here to see another year".

17

Rebound Love

"It's funny how much we give, live, and feed on the very existence of the one we love and think we need. Living in a selfish world only leads to lies, fear and deceit that we reap from one in a million human beings in this world because the purest most blissful moments of love left us on bended knee. You see, our hearts break from the feeling of being unwanted in the late nights/early mornings of the summer breeze or the dark, cold lonely nights of the winter freeze, but we stay up late texting their phones, scrolling on social media begging baby please just want me, need me anything but let me go to sleep feeling like I'm an option and not a need in this thing called life that I thought together we would lead.

Love is the most dangerous drug that we crave. We feel like we need, yet people dismiss it until actions turn to outer body displays of mental health webs that our hurt, anger and betrayal conveys and then they expect us to just leave? Yea right you thief! With each person that dealt me this drug laced with every destructive additive made me deconstruct from the very internal depths of my being."

Chris stole me from right under Kalvin's nose. I thought I was getting back to the type of man I deserved. Chris was cool. Physically appealing, early thirties, business minded...I was open, but also vulnerable. He knew it, so he pursued, or should I say preyed on me. Early on, I started to take the back seat in this relationship. I was trying to be that submissive woman. He was focused solely on his business, but I understood because I was in the middle of drafting the manuscript for this book among other projects I was working on as an entrepreneur. I just felt like I found balance in putting time into us and focusing on achieving my goals, but he was different.

I started feeling off. Not because of him. I guess I was more overwhelmed than I thought from work and life. We had a Mental Health Awareness Day at my job where I tested positive for Post Traumatic Stress Disorder (PTSD) and Anxiety...both above average test results. I needed him more than ever, but he was distracted.

On June 19, 2017, I attended a conference at Penn State University for my job. My mom went with me to get away and keep me company. She noticed I was off on the trip. I didn't know how to talk to her, but I knew I needed to open up to someone. While we were in the hotel room the night of the 20th, I felt the confidence to open up. The words wouldn't come out, but I was positioned like I had something to say. She was patient. Finally I was ready.

"Mom…"

"Yes"

"I have been feeling off recently. I don't know what I'm going through but it's different. I feel depressed all the time, but now I'm starting to actually walk myself through possible ways to commit suicide."

I don't know any mother who would think this is an easy conversation. My mom is Superwoman, so she found a way to make me feel comfortable as I opened up to her. By the end of the conversation I felt good. I knew that I was not alone in feeling this way. I was proud of myself for letting someone in before it was too late. And more importantly, it opened an even deeper bond with my mom.

June 21, 2017 was the final end to us…or so I thought. I missed his call, so he followed up with a text. I turned over to the nightstand, barely awake and responded…

"I was sleep I told you I'm at a conference. I'm not really up after midnight"

"It's ok Hun. Still wanted to try"

"I understand…I just be wanting to talk"

"Its ok have a good day"

"Have a good day baby at the conference."

***

Jun 21st, 10:33pm

"Hi"

"Hey love"

"Great day today for me…How was yours?"

"Good…I'm glad you had a good day"

"Can you talk or you still busy?"

"I've been done since 4. I've been waiting for you."

"Didn't know how long your conference was."

"Did you watch my radio show yet?"

"No. I haven't had time…Sorry. I'll watch it tonight I promise."

"It's ok I was just asking. Well I'll talk to you later. I'm glad you had a great day," I said in disappointment

"I'll watch it tonight."

"Goodnight"

Excited about his production, he quickly redirected the

conversation back to his success.

"I got 16 pts. today"

"Awesome" I responded alert yet tired and irritated.

"Call me after your conference"

"Goodnight"

"Goodnight"

***

"I don't want you to watch the show. It's been a week. I just didn't know if you watched it from the last time I mentioned it."

"Go to bed Hun lol...Now I gotta watch"

"I am I just kinda was upset it was important to me."

I guess he felt bad about not watching my show and went on my Facebook page to find the playback of the live recording I did from the studio. It had been over a week since my radio appearance. I let him know about it, sent him the recording and even tagged him in my shared post the night before of the recording. I guess he was too busy to share the excitement of my accomplishments because he was so focused on his own. That hurt. I always liked his pictures on Facebook when he got customers, commenting to tell them thank you for supporting, and telling him that he was doing a great job. I guess it was only my job to pour into him. Or maybe because I wasn't trying to go Senior

Vice President like him, so I guess my little book wasn't as important. Whatever it was, I didn't care anymore. I was clapping for myself before him and I can just keep doing the same despite his support.

I quieted my mind and starting falling asleep, but then my phone went off, so I rolled over to look at it.

"Your Facebook says single! Wow ok. Be single then. And you're hugged up with a guy in your pic with some guy lips on you?"

"I never changed my status like you"

"Goodbye Tiphane"

"What you talkin about?" I said in confusion.

"I ask you to watch my show and now you're turning this on me. Wow. And that's not a guy if you paid attention to my page like that. Always acting out when I express to you!"

And just like that I was blocked. He refused my calls. He ended our relationship over a picture I took while out with my dad at a Father's Day play with one of my older brother's closest friends from church. We broke up over a picture. All I wanted him to do was support me, but somehow this was deflected back on me.

We were over. I was already depressed and contemplated suicide and now this happened. I always covered up my hurt. Pressed toward achieving a higher goal when I was discouraged. This time I was tired. Drained in every aspect of my life. He wanted out and I wasn't going to stop him. Till this day, he still hasn't watched my radio interview.

Weeks later, I found out why I had been going through a turmoil of emotions. The journey that I set out on from the very beginning was coming full circle. I found love between my thighs in the most unconditional form possible...my unborn child.

18

My Unborn Love

"Hello my love. This was our first day together (July 6, 2017). Well our first official day. You have been in my tummy for six to seven weeks already, but I didn't know you were there. I was so sick and weak; I had to go to the doctor to see why. After hearing my symptoms I was asked to pee in a cup. I walked back to my designated room at the medical center thinking I would be waiting a while. Two minutes later the doctor returned and before I could brace myself she told me I am pregnant with you. I cried so hard and I felt alone, but for the first time I wasn't because you were there. They gave me the pregnancy test that showed you were officially forming in my tummy. I didn't know what to feel or think, I just cried. I called your dad and cried in his ear. Unbeknownst to me, he was expecting you. Today I spent the day talking to your Nani, Pop. Pop-Pop, aunts and uncles to let them know you are coming into our lives. I am proud God chose me to be your mommy. I don't know what to do yet, but I will learn. I know that you have an awesome village around you and you will be loved by so many. I pray God's favor and protection over your life. That you will put on the full armor of God starting now. That neither sickness nor diseases come nigh your dwelling. That God anoint you with the musical gifts of your grandfather, the strength and spiritual wisdom of your grandmother, the resilience and ability to bring any vision to fruition like your mother, and the competitive drive of your father. That all things happen for a reason, so I will be strong in the Lord and give you life. I love you my little blessing. You are the love that came from between my thighs. Not in the way I was expecting, but in the way that was intended for my life."

Stay tuned for *The Love Between My Thighs: A Journey to Motherhood and Beyond*

Outro

It seems like every time life hits, God sends my nephew to the rescue. Every heartache, bitterness, or depressed moment that I have endured since 2015 he has showed up. This time was no different. He climbed up the kitchen island with his Wendy's happy meal and started eating his chicken nuggets and fries. He told me I needed to eat, and I told him I wasn't hungry. He started feeding me French fries one by one with silly airplane noises, making me open my mouth to receive the French fries. When he finished, he came closer and started playing in my hair. He told me that he wanted to do my hair so I could look perfect. I began to heal, but God had another journey in store for me...

Epilogue

All this time I thought I was fighting to practice waiting for that helpmate God was sending me. I thought that I was keeping myself to acknowledge and respect the spiritual confounds in which I was raised. I thought I was delaying my personal gratifications of the flesh for a greater reward in the end. And while all of that sounded great, I realized that I first needed to learn what all of that was for. I may not have held my celibacy, but I did finally learn that love does not lie between my thighs. I'm starting to actually understand sex, what it means, and the impact it has on the two people who connect. I'm talking beyond spiritual bonds and strongholds. I realized that even if I moved on, even if I became celibate, even if I upheld my spiritual commitments to God, life would repeat itself if I first did not have the epiphany within myself that love is bigger than the oceanic feel between my thighs. I no longer feel guilty for thinking about sex, or having sex. Not because I'm not a Christian, but because I got it for myself. Not relying on man or judgment to help me see the relief I need to mend the wounds of my heart from so many acts of *Love Between My Thighs*, fingers, lips, dicks and the like. But today I'm free, not just from my body, but my mind.

Each of these men was a necessary part of my life to teach me what I know now. I still won't be perfect, but at least now I'll feel good from the inside out knowing what I know. My heart will battle the past because our minds rehash more bad memories than good, but consciousness is half the battle. I know I was built as a soldier who survives war.

When we deal with a breakup or tragedy, we only think about the scars on our hearts, but what about the ones that are deeper? It's more to hurt than just a woman's heart. The distractions of love make you feel differently.

This was me, a valued prize still stuck in a see-through box. Still waiting for the crane to save me so that I can be the prize someone wins. However, I have learned that the best jewels are the hardest to catch. They have the roughest edges and they take more time to smooth. This time, I'm waiting for the man to see me from afar, be excited in the beginning about the enticing prize before his eyes and live each day with him enjoying his winnings.

I realize that life is all about perspective. Instead of feeling stuck between wanting to free myself so I too can stand on the other side of that window, or wanting to hide and bury myself even deeper into the masses, I have decided to wait for the right person to invest in the crane. The person who will understand the value of the prize he wants, and will strategize how to get the prize out. To take his time with the process so that the prize will successfully drop in the slot where he could pick me up and take home his winnings. It isn't a bad thing to wait.

Takeaways

R eserve your dating life for people actively involved in the growth process.

Healthy people attract and find other healthy people so take back your life, own it, and be happy and free!

Queens promote health, wealth, and an assured self, so let's get healthy, spend smarter/save more, and empower ourselves so that we can gain the confidence we need to understand the value we have!

"Beautiful women with beautiful minds that have beautiful hearts produce beautiful things" ~Tiphane L.M. Purnell
So keep yourself beautiful from the inside out and you can never go wrong.

Different perspectives in 2017. Waiting on my King while serving The King of Kings!

My story is filled with broken pieces, poor decisions, and some ugly truths. But, it's also filled with major comebacks, peace in my soul and grace that saved my life.

Queens stop dating potential and date reality!

Sis, you've always fought for others. This will be the year that others fight for you.

Don't just wait for a man. Wait for a Man of God. Be prepared for the perks and pitfalls of the difference. #dating #writersbag

Before Eve came along, Adam was alone, but he was not lonely. Understand the difference Queens!

You are AMAZING! Did you know that???
"Maturity requires self awareness, but this is not to be confused with self-absorption." Self awareness is acknowledging who you are by looking beyond outward appearance to the heart. Ladies let's learn to LOVE our mirrors, and accept who you are inside and out!

Healing is not comfortable. The discomfort and hurt it part of the process. Don't run from healing, run into it.

If you do not wait to have sex until marriage, you will still end up waiting in the long run. You will get tired of giving your body, emotions, and spirit away to be shared. You will realize that you have given your heart to people who never even deserved a hug from you. By the time you realize this, you will have wished you waited.

All scars heal with time, but time does not heal all scars. Put in the work to heal.

163

The closure you seek can set you back years. The real closure is when you make the decision to chose yourself.

Closure happens when you decide to close the door and never look back into the same situation again.

Love waits to give, but lust can't wait to get. The next time someone says they "love you" check yourself. Don't give 100% of yourself without getting 100% of them.

We have to do a better job at protecting our visions, dreams, and our hearts, so that we can keep our wealth secure.

The season of singleness is a preparation period, not a desperation period.

Believing the all the positive traits that make up that fierce Queen within starts with your mindset.

Book Club Guide

The Love Between My Thighs is an excellent book to read with other women to ignite discussion on various aspects that affect a woman's life mentally, physically, emotionally, and spiritually when dealing with relationships whether platonic or romantic. Below you will find discussion questions to spark intentional and engaging dialogue among a group of women. If you want to spice up the conversation, invite some men to exchange perspectives on love, life and relationships.

1. What first came to mind when you read the title "The Love Between My Thighs?"

2. Discovering yourself is a journey. What would you have done different before and/or after your first?

3. What resonated with you the most when reading this book? Why do you think it is important for women to reflect and heal this part of themselves?

4. Share your favorite quote/passage from the book.
    Why did this quote/passage stand out?

5. What feelings did this book evoke in you?

6. If you got the chance to ask the author of this book
    one question, what would it be?

7. What gaps do you wish the author had filled in?

Success
Resources

If you are truly ready to get successful results on your transformation from destruction to destiny, we have some resources that will help you on your journey.

The Pen-It Project™
If you are ready to tell your story, I am ready to coach your through the steps to publish your story for the world to read. The Bible tells us, "The pen is mightier than the sword," so I challenge you all to release your hurt with pen and paper and get your healing and freedom through helping others.

Success Dealers International™
Group Coaching Program
Private Coaching Program
Boot Camp
Online Masterclass Series
Business Planning and Execution

Future Projects
The Love Between My Thighs: The Journey to Motherhood and Beyond©
32©
Unstoppable: Turning Fears, Frustrations, and Failures into Fortunes©

Private Coaching
Work one-on-one with me to release the scars beyond your heart and set your mind free from the internal war of past hurt and pain.

Sign up at successdealersintl@gmail.com to transform your life and/or business today!

About the Author

Tiphane` L.M. Purnell is a cutting edge, millennial empowerment powerhouse, ready to give you the hard-core business, branding, and relationship coaching you need to curate your dreams into profitable realities.

Selected as the 2011 Business of the Year from the Delmarva Chapter of the Home-Based Business Chamber of Commerce, and nominated as Best Female Business in Delaware through the National Black Guide; she is on a mission to be results driven and accept no excuses in realizing your dreams in your personal and business life.

THE LOVE BETWEEN MY THIGHS

TIPHANE` L.M. PURNELL

Made in the USA
Middletown, DE
01 March 2020